Wicca for beginners

A Guide to Becoming Wiccan. Understand Witchcraft and Wicca Religion and Mysteries of Spells, Herbal Magic, Moon Magic, Crystal Magic. A starter kit for Wiccan Practitioner.

Linda Candles

Text Copyright © Linda Candles

All rights reserved. No part of this guide may be reproduced in any form without permission in writing from the publisher except in the case of brief quotations embodied in critical articles or reviews.

Legal & Disclaimer

The information contained in this book and its contents is not designed to replace or take the place of any form of medical or professional advice; and is not meant to replace the need for independent medical, financial, legal or other professional advice or services, as may be required. The content and information in this book has been provided for educational and entertainment purposes only.

The content and information contained in this book has been compiled from sources deemed reliable, and it is accurate to the best of the Author's knowledge, information and belief. However, the Author cannot guarantee its accuracy and validity and cannot be held liable for any errors and/or omissions. Further, changes are periodically made to this book as and when needed. Where appropriate and/or necessary, you must consult a professional (including but not limited to your doctor, attorney, financial advisor or such other professional advisor) before using any of the suggested remedies, techniques, or information in this book.

Upon using the contents and information contained in this book, you agree to hold harmless the Author from and against any damages, costs, and expenses, including any legal fees potentially resulting from the application of any of the information provided by this book. This disclaimer applies to any loss, damages or injury caused by the use and application, whether directly or indirectly, of any advice or information presented, whether for breach of contract, tort, negligence, personal injury, criminal intent, or under any other cause of action.

You agree to accept all risks of using the information presented inside this book.

You agree that by continuing to read this book, where appropriate and/or necessary, you shall consult a professional (including but not limited to your doctor, attorney, or financial advisor or such other advisor as needed) before using any of the suggested remedies, techniques, or information in this book.

Table of Contents

Book Description 1

Introduction 3

Chapter 1 Common Misconceptions about Wicca 11

Chapter 2 The wiccan deities 31

Chapter 3 Wicca in our modern world 47

Chapter 4 Wicca and Satanism 55

Chapter 5 The Campaign Against Witches 71

Chapter 6 Sabbats and Esbats 79

Chapter 7 The Wiccan Elements 87

Chapter 8 Wiccan Tools Commonly Found on the Altar 91

Chapter 9 Consecrating Your Tools 97

Chapter 10 Joining a Coven 103

Chapter 11 Becoming a Solo Practitioner of Wicca 107

Chapter 12 Love Spells 113

Chapter 13 Wealth spells 127

Conclusion 137

Book Description

Wicca has had its ups and downs in the magical community, booming in popularity shortly after its beginning, and today in full force as magic and other nature-focused practices enter the popular culture once again. This acceptance of magic and pagan influenced religions in recent years has added a sense of validity to these practices in a world gradually abandoning materialism and atheism. The ideas of duo theism and polytheism have been practiced for many centuries and are well-documented in writing. Wicca draws much of its inspiration from these pre-Christian cultures and their practices, while also applying the twentieth-century lens on the organization and initiations, similar to Victorian-era hierarchal societies.

With this new boom in acceptance of nature worship and magical practice Wicca has seen a rebirth as seekers of all walks of life search for insight into the subtle forces all around us. Communion with nature and other intelligence is a central focus for Wicca and many other of these movements. This book's purpose is to help the seeker begin their journey on a natural path, to empower themselves to make their own spiritual choices and walk the path safely.

While many may look at Wicca and scoff at the dress and history of the religion, the practices and rituals within the Wiccan sphere are very potent. This is not a live action role play or fantasy acting.

These forces are very real and the potency of these forces should be taken lightly. Anyone who has ever been curious about magic essentially has already begun their path. Rarely does any individual who starts this journey turn back unchanged. Communion with nature and its forces should not be for fun or treated as just another weekend activity.

These things are very real and should be treated with respect and humility when approached by the beginner or the adept. There is danger and you will change, whether the changes are subtle or dramatic. Do not approach these practices heedlessly and be sure to take the necessary precaution when you are engaging with these forces. This is not a hobby, but a lifestyle that aims to build relationships with spirits, in nature and all around us.

Approaching magical techniques and rituals can be confusing or even intimidating at first; this is to be expected. Our western society has effectively eliminated communion with spirits from the popular sphere. It is regarded as 'not real' since it cannot be proven scientifically. There are some things science cannot prove and our society is coming to terms with that. Many of the promises science offered in the past decades have not come to fruition.

Introduction

Magic is accessible to everyone, and this book will take you down the path towards comfortably using it to improve your health and confidence, open your heart to love, increase your money, wealth, and abundance, keep negativity away from your doorstep, and ensure many blessings for your future.

What Is Wicca?

The word Wicca originates from the Old English and means simply, "witch". Older Germanic languages attribute additional meanings such as **foretell, speak, and divine** (as in divination).

But what does a witch do? We may have been taught to connect witchcraft with darker things such as evil, Satanism, and manipulation, but only the last word is correct. A witch **does** manipulate things but only within themselves. Then, we resonate the effects of that change outward into the world.

There are many forms of modern Pagan practice; Wicca is one of them.

The birth of Wicca as a modern religion can be traced back to the writings of a retired British civil servant, Gerald Gardner—in fact, there is an entire branch of Wiccan practice devoted to him called Gardnerian Wicca. He published his definitive book on the subject, **Witchcraft Today** back in 1954. Gardner also founded a coven—essentially a prayer/workgroup for witches, numbering anywhere from four to 40 members or more—and several members of his coven went on to publish books on the subject of witchcraft and magical living.

In Gardnerian and other traditional practices, a coven is led by a priest and priestess, who oversee the ceremonial Sabbath rituals and often represent the god and goddess during these rituals. They are also in charge of educating newer members of the coven and helping members move upward in the steps of a witch's formal education and life—wiccaning (naming), handfasting, croning, etc.

The Wiccan Rede and the Threefold Law

Here we have one of many examples of similarities between Wicca and Judeo-Christian faiths. The Wiccan Rede is essentially the Golden Rule, worded as such: "Do what ye will, that it harm none." There is, so far, no evidence of this rede (rede means guidance or wisdom) in Ancient European pagan practices, but it is believed to have been penned by one of Gardner's coven members, Doreen Valiente.

The Wiccan Rede is in itself at the core of Wiccan philosophy—when it comes to spell-casting and daily life, a Wiccan makes a concerted effort to cause no harm. At the very least, malevolent intent is never a part of a Wiccan's practice—at best, this outlook causes them to live their lives with a purpose to add positivity to the world, and not increase the already-present negativity. Examples of this include volunteering, living green and recycling, fostering, and taking time for self-care and reflection. There is a touch of Buddhism and Eastern philosophy in this mindset, and while admittedly, it may very well be impossible to go through one's day without accidentally stepping on a bug or using single-use plastic, the goal of the Wiccan Rede is to try one's best and never **intentionally** harm. It has been said that "white magic is pretty; but black magic works," but at the true heart of Wicca lies the belief that by following the natural laws and mimicking them in one's magical practices, one can achieve peace and happiness in life.

The Threefold Law states that whatever you do comes back to you, times three. Think of a pond when you throw a stone into it, and the subsequent ripples that slowly emerge to touch the shoreline. This basic tenet holds you to be accountable for your actions; whatever you do has consequences, so live mindfully and responsibly.

But the natural world can be violent sometimes, right? True. The natural world involves catastrophic storms, predator animals hunting prey animals, baby loggerhead turtles marching stoically towards the inland rather than the sea. Wicca takes us to task for being mindful, thoughtful creatures—it asks us to revere and respect the natural world, and make the conscious decision not to add to its disasters or calamities. A Wiccan will stop his or her car to help a turtle across the road, and will often be a more empathic, supportive parent to their children. Wiccans are merely human, however, and so additional words have been written to ensure followers of Wicca do not abuse the power that they've learned to harness: **"By the power of three, to cause no one harm nor to cause harm to me."** All spellcraft must be devoid of harmful intent, or else simply—it is not Wicca.

A Faith of Acceptance

One of the things that draw people to Wicca is the fact that anyone can join. Men and women of any background, gender identity or sexuality are welcome. In addition, both the god and the goddess are recognized within each of us—instead of faith and ritual being highly gender-restrictive, it's understood that the god and the goddess represent the polarity and flow of energy within each being on Earth. Men can be caring fathers and express their emotions; women can be mighty and fierce and still considered feminine. Practitioners of Wicca are taught to understand that they both manifest the god and the goddess as well as learn from them on a daily basis.

In addition to accepting all who would want to enter the ways of Wicca, the Wiccan faith does not dictate how that new follower should practice his or her faith; many Wiccans prefer to practice in the privacy of their homes, while others still prefer to find a coven or larger community group to celebrate the Sabbaths with (Sabbaths are holidays throughout the year as well as full moon gatherings). While some Wiccans consider themselves monotheists and look at the power of the universe as a single deity, and all of the gods' and goddesses' **aspects** of that greater power, others consider themselves polytheists. Some Wiccans find themselves called to the Egyptian gods, others pray to Celtic ones, and still others to Asian nature spirits. The choice is up to the practitioner, and no other Wiccan judges the next for how they follow their faith.

Living in the "Now"

Unlike other faiths, Wicca doesn't use threats to coerce its followers to practice better behavior. Life is not considered a proving-ground for a VIP-only afterlife. Life is the lesson, the daily chance to live well and to live in harmony with one's surroundings. There is forgiveness in each day—just as the Sun will always rise, so does a Wiccan realize that there is always time for a change for the better, and their connection with the god/goddess and nature can help ease them through difficult times, and towards a better life.

This is not to say that Wiccans don't believe in an afterlife. The afterlife is often referred to as "The Summerlands," and it does keep with other faiths in believing that the afterlife is a place of gentle repose, more forgiving than one's mortal life, but Wicca holds that all retire there in equality and peace.

The History of Wicca and Witchcraft

The name Wicca comes from old Anglo - Saxon word "wicce" meaning wisdom. Wicca as a cult is a form of Neo - Pagan Witchcraft. These terms are in many ways similar yet they hold some significant differences. One can be a Wiccan without practicing witchcraft and one can be a witch and practice Witchcraft without following the path of Wicca.

The history of Wicca and Witchcraft is full of misconceptions, half-truths, and prejudice and most of it started in the middle ages. We have all heard and read of how the Inquisition used to pursue and try, torture and kill people accused of practicing witchcraft.

Witchcraft starts more or less with the beginning of the first human civilization. Witchcraft was also known as "The Craft of the Wise." A witch can be both male and female and they all honored the Spirit of Nature. They had a vast amount of knowledge of herbs, medicines, and food and life was greatly focused around establishing a connection with Mother Earth.

Archeological discoveries have found 40.000 years old evidence of Paleolithic people worshiping a Hunter God and a Fertility Goddess. Wicca places emphasis on spiritual peace and respect for Nature which nurtures you and gives you life. Witches also served as mediators between the physical and the spiritual world.

Gerald Gardner was a British civil servant who claimed that he joined an existing Wicca Coven in 1939. Later on, in 1949 he wrote a book about Wicca "High Magick's Aid". According to Gardner, Wicca is a religion that recognizes both Goddess and a Horned God of the Ancient North European Pagan Beliefs. Regardless of such claims, however, we know that Wicca is a modern day take on a religion tracing its roots as early as the first human civilizations.

Chapter 1 Common Misconceptions about Wicca

Approximately one and a half million pagans are living in the US according to a 2014 study, and approximately one hundred thousand living in the UK, not to mention pagans living and practicing their faiths in Scandinavia, South America, Canada, Italy, and other countries of the EU. Even though those numbers are impressive, modern paganism (also known as "neo-paganism") is a collection of faiths that are considered a minority in comparison to Abrahamic religions such as Christianity, Judaism, and Islam.

What happens most often when you have a majority and a minority? Misconceptions—and what we don't understand we often tend to fear, or even spread rumors about.

The Pentacle and Pentagram. A pentagram is a five-pointed star; it can be inverse or right-side up. A pentacle is a five-pointed star set within a circle. While some believe these are the signs of Satanist beliefs, nothing could be further from the truth.

A pentagram with the star's single point right-side up symbolizes humanity. If you look at one, you can see a figure standing tall, arms and legs outstretched. The pentagram and pentacle serve as a tool to remind us of the power and potential of humanity. As children of the god and goddess, we are imbued with sacred gifts that help us to connect to ourselves, nature, and the universe beyond should we choose to learn about and use these gifts.

A pentagram is often the starting point for ancient talismans, such as those one would find in the Key of Solomon. In ancient times, these talismans were used for purposes ranging from drawing upon the power of the Moon to calling angels to help with aid, to extending life and strengthening one's health.

A pentagram with the two bottom-most points' right-side up is often mistaken for the sign of the Devil. The Devil is a construct of Christianity's teachings, and not part of any pagan practice. The so-called "upside down" pentagram invokes the wild spirit of nature by showing us a horned animal, as well as reminding us of the Horned God—a pagan deity representative of nature, hunting, and the beasts we share the Earth with. Some pagans and Wiccans use the reversed pentagram when they want to get closer to nature.

The ancient symbol of the pentagram is also found and used extensively in tarot, particularly in the iconic Rider-Waite tarot deck first published in 1909.

Wiccans (and Pagans) Are Overly Sexual. This too is a common misconception. The difference here is that Wiccans understand sex is not connected with "sin"—in fact, being human by nature is not a sinful thing. We are all capable of malice, to some extent, and we must learn to live responsibly as adults—especially if we are not taught to do so as children. In the pagan faith, sex is a vital part of being human, but only consensually. It is to be respected as a sacred act, even if in a casual moment. Sexuality gives us life, but more importantly, it gives us touch, intimacy, and human connection. That being said, sex is not a necessary part of any pagan faith, including Wicca—being celibate is respected just as much as being polyamorous—but when sex between two adults occurs, it is done with respect, and always consent.

Wiccans Cast Spells. This misconception is true! Often the image that is conjured (pun intended) is quite different than the actual practice. A Wiccan casts a spell with a very specific purpose in mind and does so after some research, preparation, and a peaceful heart. Most importantly, a Wiccan casts a spell knowing there will be consequences for that magic released into the world, and would never cast a spell that would bring harm into an already chaotic world.

Think of a spell not as "magic" in the Judeo-Christian sense, but as a tool of focus. Just as mantras, prayers, therapy, and manifestation help us achieve greater things in our lives, so does magic for pagans and Wiccans. Humans are tool-using creatures, and magic is just one of those tools.

Wiccans Are Satanists. This is probably the most common myth. Wiccans do not believe in the Devil or Satan as a deity; these are Christian ideas. There is, however, a religion called Satanism, and it's more concerned with how a person acts and treats other people than anything else, but it is definitely not a pagan faith, nor is it Wicca.

Wiccans Conjure Demons. This edge of the supernatural world can be a little scary, admittedly, but no self-respecting Wiccan is keen on dabbling in conjuring beings that frankly nobody understands particularly well. While many Wiccans and pagans do believe in the supernatural world—ghosts, angels, and other things that might or might not go bump in the night—they do not actively try to recruit them to get the housework done or wilt their neighbor's roses. The Wiccan Rede, the Threefold Law, and just plain, old common sense recommends otherwise!

Wiccans Always Wear Black. This is perhaps a silly myth, but still relatively active thanks to television and movies depicting witches. Wiccans wear whatever they like; some do prefer black, as black is a color of protection and shielding. Some Wiccans become very attuned to what is around them—including the energy of others—and black can help dampen that, somewhat. Other Wiccans prefer wearing white or lighter colors during a ritual, and still, others wear colors to match the current season of the year. Some Wiccans prefer to wear nothing at all, going "skyclad" during rituals—but this is either in the privacy of their home or among consenting members of their group or coven.

The Triple Goddess

In pagan faiths, including Wicca, the Goddess is viewed as the focal point of life. She walks with us through our entire lives, mirroring every step we take. Additionally, the Triple Goddess reflects the world itself—she **is** the world, as shown in the changing seasons, the phases of the Moon, the ebb and flow of tides, and the life cycle of every living thing.

Throughout human history, we have had examples of Triple Goddesses, such as Hera, the Greek wife of Zeus who is shown in three forms: a young girl, an adult woman, and an elderly woman. Another example of the Triple Goddess concept can be found in Ancient Middle Eastern texts, which name three goddesses: Al-Uzza, Al-at, and Manat. Each represents a different point in life; their names can be translated as **the star, the woman, the crone.**

Curiously, Gardner did not mention the Triple Goddess in his first book, and only briefly in his second book, **The Meaning of Witchcraft**. After a visit with a friend on the island of Majorca, Gardner wrote an undated essay in which he elaborates greatly on the concept of the Triple Goddess, and finds similarities between the triple aspects and the Christian "Son, Father, and Holy Ghost." He also sees a comforting, healing aspect to the Crone, or third cycle of the goddess, and prefers to call her "rebirth."

The Maiden

The Maiden represents the beginnings of life and can be seen in the example when the Moon is in its waxing to full phase. She reminds us of our potential and our promise; she epitomizes hope in all things. She is the seed that waits beneath the cold soil in winter and the nourishing water that comes from a spring thaw. When thunder rumbles in the sky, she reminds us that rain is necessary for all things to grow.

The maiden also represents one's life force separate from sexuality or sexual connection. The Maiden may or not necessarily be a virgin, but she is at a stage in her life where life is too busy and full of learning for her to begin to put down roots and start a family. Those who are celibate, single, or simply focused on other paths in their life can be aided by the Maiden in their pursuits.

The Maiden represents the adventurer, the lone sailor taking their ship out to an uncharted horizon, or the hunter entering an unmapped wood for the first time. Pray to the Maiden for guidance when beginning something new. The Maiden herself is not new—in Wicca, life is circular, always ending and always beginning again. The Maiden rises from the ashes of the phoenix-like Crone and carries great wisdom with her.

A list of maiden goddesses:

Artemis. A Greek goddess, Artemis is an expert hunter and a symbol of chosen celibacy. She prefers a simple life surrounded by nature. She has domain over the waxing moon. Pray to Artemis for courage, and peace during times of solitude. She also adamantly defends women who have suffered abuse at the hands of men.

Artemis is a great protector of wildlife, and those who work in this field can also find it useful to pray to her.

In summer, a gift of wildflower honey makes a perfect offering; in winter, red wine or any berry-colored juice poured over a bowl of snow.

The Roman aspect of Artemis is **Diana.** Oak groves are sacred to her, and like Artemis, her symbol is the bow.

Artemis' favored colors are red, white, green, and silver.

Blodeuwedd. A Welsh goddess (her name means "flower-faced"), Blodeuwedd was brought into the world by two magicians in an effort to keep the seasons going after a curse was placed on a young king. She represents the balance in nature. Pray to her when you need balance in your life, especially in relationships.

Broom, meadowsweet, and oak are sacred to her.

Bodeuwedd's favored colors are green and white.

Freya. A Norse goddess, Freya has domain over many things, including love, sex, sorcery, and battle. She represents the vitality of the life force and its potential realized. Pray to her when your life is lacking in richness and passion, or when you would like to open yourself to love. She is also very helpful to women in labor.

Freya keeps two gray cats and as such, gray cats are favored by her. Her sword is carved with runes for power, fertility, and birth.

Freya's favored colors are green, gold, and red.

Parvati. A Hindu goddess, Parvati symbolizes courage during adversity. She is a gentle goddess (in this aspect), and carries a message with the symbol, or **mudra,** displayed by her right hand that says, "Do not fear anyone or anything." She is proof that strength can be quiet, and not brash or showy. Pray to Parvati for courage and the strength to endure, as well as renewed belief in your goodness, and your abilities to succeed.

Parvati's favored colors are yellow and copper.

Persephone (also known as Kore). Persephone is a goddess who shifts through all of the phases of the Triple Goddess as the Wheel of the Year turns. In her Maiden aspect, she represents those who are wise beyond their years and those who are called "old souls". She can be seen in the young person quietly at work or play, disturbing no one, lost in thought and contemplation. She also represents widows, widowers, and anyone who grieves for a loved one. Pray to Persephone in times of reflection, loss, or when you just need a supportive, listening ear. Remember that Persephone rises from the Underworld to bring spring to our world, every year. She is a champion of hope.

Persephone's favored colors are black, white, purple (think of crocuses), and pale green.

Oshun. A Nigerian goddess brought to the United States by slaves and worshipped there as an Orisha (La Caridad del Cobre is her "saint name"), Oshun represents the vivacity of youth and the life of the party. She rules over wealth, sex, love, and fun. She protects dancers and artists. She laughs when she is sad or angry, and cries tears of joy when she's delighted. She can heal the most brokenhearted and lift up the most downtrodden. Pray to Oshun when you need an outpouring of love from the cosmos, and she will give you what you asked for, manyfold.

It stands to reason that you should always be respectful when praying to the gods, but always be respectful to Oshun. One of her favorite offerings is honey—but you must taste it yourself before giving it to her, as someone tried to poison her honey once. She also loves pumpkin, champagne, and yellow flowers.

Oshun's favored colors are yellow and gold.

The Mother

The Mother goddess represents the apex of life and the full moon. Many of us automatically think of the Mother aspect when we think of the word "goddess"; throughout human history, the vision of a mothering, nurturing, and fertile figure is iconic and everlasting because the Earth itself embodies her. The soil and water nourish us as a mother nurses her newborn child; the skies bring rain that helps everything around us grow, and every spring the world seems reborn.

The Mother goddess exemplifies the pinnacle of our journey when we realize our potential and enjoy the fruits of our labor—metaphorically and literally.

The goddess in this aspect resonates through us all, regardless of gender, fertility issues, or disabilities. Each of us has potential to be realized; each one of us was born with a seed growing within our hearts and souls. The Mother goddess is there to help us see it awaken and bear fruit because that is the purpose of our life's path.

A list of mother goddesses:

Arianrhod. A Celtic goddess, Arianrhod's domains are fertility, rebirth, and the lessons and tapestry of fate. She symbolizes the ever-turning Wheel of the Year, and as such, a silver wheel is both the translation of her name and her token. She not only presides over the birth of new souls into the world but leads the departed to their eternal rest in the Summerlands.

Those who work with fabric, divination, or as guides can benefit from praying to Arianrhod. She also represents the power of will in the face of arrogance and will help her followers be strong in times of duress. Ivy and birch trees are sacred to her.

Arianrhod's favored colors are white and silver.

Bast (or Pasht). Bast might at first seem an unlikely mother goddess, but in fact, Ancient Egyptian women would pray to her for children while wearing amulets inscribed with kittens equal to the number of babies they wanted to birth. Bast is a feline goddess and cats are sacred to her. She also protects the household, keeping evil from it as a cat chases pests away.

In addition to helping would-be parents and households, Bast protects firefighters. This belief stems from the Egyptian belief that a cat could put out the flames of a home by running through it and drawing the fire out into the street, thus saving the house.

Bast's alternate name, Pasht, is the etymological root for the word **pleasure**. She presides over the joys of life and everything that makes life worth living. Pray to Bast when you are seeking joy, or to thank her for something joyful that has come into your life. You can plant catnip, or any herb associated with the Sun, in your garden to welcome Bast into your home.

Bast's favored colors are red, yellow, gold, and white.

Brigid. Brigid's domains are many and include the fires of both the hearth and the forge, the cauldron of inspiration, birth, fertility, and creativity. Anyone who creates—with their words, ideas, hammer, brush, or hands can turn to Brigid when the wells of inspiration run dry, and she will relight the fires of your forge.

Brigid is most celebrated on Imbolc, a Sabbath in February. She shares this day with **Oya**, a Nigerian goddess whose domain is fire, rainbows, lightning, and cemeteries.

Demeter. This Greek goddess presides over agriculture, grain, fertility, the harvest, and sacred law. She is believed to have taught humanity the art of growing corn and with this shares a syncretization with the Native American **Corn Goddess**, as well as the Aztec goddess **Chicomecoatl** and the Zulu goddess **Inkosazana**. Wreaths made of corn, as well as snakes and pigs, are all sacred to her. Pray to Demeter for a good harvest—be it from your land and garden, or from a project you have worked hard at. Share your yields at her altar in thanks. Wheat, acorns, and honey are sacred to her.

Demeter's favored colors are green, gold, dark brown, and blue.

Frigg. This Norse goddess was called upon to bring children into a union. Her domain is divination, and she masterfully practiced the art of **seidr** or determining a person's fate. Pray to Frigg when you need help with listening to your intuition, and she will guide you. Ravens, hawks, and falcons are sacred to her, as well as the plant, mistletoe.

Frigg's favored colors are black, green, and red.

Isis. This Egyptian goddess has so much love to give to the world. Her domains include marriage, music, and magic, as well as protection of the natural world. She represents empathy and understanding and is said to open her heart to the downtrodden, regardless of circumstance. Pray to Isis when you are feeling hopeless or lost; pray to her to share your happiness when it returns to your life. Cinnamon, sandalwood, and oranges are sacred to her. Isis is also a protector of children and our beloved dead.

Isis' favored colors are black, red, silver, gold, and cobalt blue.

Inari. This Japanese god/goddess is considered to be neither male nor female (or both) and presides over agriculture and the bountiful aspect of life. The Shinto religion, from which this **kami**, or nature spirit, originates, is quite supportive of people from across the world lending homage and praise to their deities, and so Inari enjoys a huge following worldwide. Inari's messengers are foxes called **kitsune**, and to see a fox is considered very lucky indeed. Inari inspires the artist and the creator and watches dutifully over the farmer. Inari encourages us to count our blessings and be earnest in all of our endeavors. The message "act with good intention, always" is one that Inari strives to teach us. Pray to Inari for guidance when your path seems obscured, and watch your visions and dreams for **kitsune** to guide you.

Inari's favored color is vibrant red, as are the gates that lead to his/her shrines.

Yemaya. This Nigerian goddess presides over the ocean, wealth, and motherhood. She is mighty, her depths uncharted, and she represents the power of creation in the universe. She is the sister of **Oshun**, and like her, she was also carried to the Americas by the slaves, where worship of her continued via the syncretization with Catholic saints (she is also known as "Our Lady of Regla".)

She is deeply protective of her children and can cure infertility in women. Similar to the feminine aspects of the moon tarot card,

Yemaya represents feminine wisdom and mystery. She guides us to have faith in the secrets of life; not everything is for us to know right away, if ever. Pray to Yemaya when you need to recharge your faith, and she will send you motherly love and reassurance.

Seashells and silver objects are sacred to Yemaya. Share some of your best meals with her as she loves rich foods. Watermelon is a favorite treat.

Yemaya's favored colors are blue, silver, and white.

The Crone

The Crone represents the ending of life, as well as its new beginning. She is the survivor and the phoenix; the wise woman and the shaman. She is ageless, timeless, and often manifests in young people who have to endure hardships, such as patients of childhood cancer. She teaches us that the ending of stories is not always marked with sadness—they are merely a new beginning, blessed with knowledge and a gentle joyfulness.

In many ways, the Crone brings as much life to the world as the Mother does; as a tree succumbs to the forest floor, it eventually becomes home to the life there. As an animal breathes its last breath, it becomes nourishment for other animals as well as the soil. The circle of life feeds itself and creates new life, eternally an ouroboros (an ancient symbol of a snake or serpent eating its tail, signifying infinity and the cycle of birth and death).

The Crone is the dark moon and the mysteries of life; she teaches us deep magic and prophecies, as well as patience and strength.

A list of crone goddesses:

Baba Yaga. A Russian and Lithuanian goddess, Baba Yaga teaches us to be thankful and to have a (sometimes dark) sense of humor. She is fully satisfied in her capacity as a wise, old woman who has reaped life's yields of experience and wisdom. She also teaches us to use our gifts wisely and frugally; with Baba Yaga watching over you, you will never go hungry. Pray to Baba Yaga whenever you need a crone's dose of wisdom. Share a bit of your morning multigrain bagel with her, and give thanks for all that you have.

Wheat, corn, and chickens are all sacred to Baba Yaga.

Baba Yaga's favored colors are white, red, and golden brown.

Hecate. This Greek goddess originally presided over magic, witchcraft, the spirit world, the night, and the dark moon, but has, throughout human history, also evolved to be a champion of marginalized people. She represents the underdog and the rebellion; the tides of change that topple the towers of those who would use their power for harm. Pray to Hecate for a great number of things, and she will guide you: in learning your craft as a Wiccan, in living a thoughtful, meaningful life, in seeing the truth in things, and in connecting to the spirit world. Pray to Hecate on election day to make the right choice for the future;

pray to her to have the courage to let go of your prejudices and become a better person. Be humble before Hecate, and she will lift you up in her heavenly arms.

Black dogs, horses, owls, and snakes are sacred to Hecate, as well as keys and crossroads.

Hecate's favored color is black.

Hel. A Norse goddess, Hel represents great compassion in death. In Norse mythology, a "straw death" was a death that occurred anywhere but in combat. Instead of to the warrior's afterlife, Valhalla, those who died a straw death went to be cared for by Hel, in Niflheim.

Hel teaches us that death is an unavoidable part of life; she also teaches us that truth will always come out, eventually, and to be truthful in our lives and practices. Hel can also teach us the great art of stillness—in contemplation, great truths can be realized, and understood. She is very much a meditative goddess, and not at all frightening. She is patient with her followers and imparts gentle wisdom upon them.

It is said that when praying to her, she will reach her hand to you. Hel's image is half flesh, half skeleton, and the hand she extends to you is her skeletal one. By taking this hand and kissing it, you ensure that she will teach you compassion. Hel is known for her compassion to all living things, regardless of ailment or deformity, and you should show her the same compassion.

Hel's symbols are bones and dried roses. She enjoys tea, wine, and apples as offerings.

Hel's favored colors are black and white.

Kali. A Hindu goddess, Kali represents the inevitability of time; in fact, the root of her name is the word for time. The death that Kali brings us is not physical death, but the death of the ego, and the attachment to material things. Pray to Kali for guidance when you need to reconnect with your true purpose, and when life has become a meaningless chase for money and material objects. Despite Kali's dangerous reputation, she is an extraordinarily compassionate goddess and cares greatly for her children. Kali also presides over celibacy, and those who practice this can take comfort in her guidance.

Roses and rosewater are sacred to Kali, as are swords, honey, and peacock feathers.

Kali's favored colors are black, purple, and red.

Morrigan. The Ancient Celts so revered this Celtic goddess that they believed she would revive their dead from the battlefield. The Morrigan (as she is commonly referred to) is indeed a powerful goddess, and she recruits her followers—often by guiding them through a series of tests or challenges in life. It is said that to pray to the Morrigan for strength is to invite a period of strife into your life, but that once you emerge victorious from this trial by fire, you will be stronger than you have ever been before.

The Morrigan teaches us that we are warriors, capable of triumphing over whatever tries to beat us. She also teaches us to be humble in our victories, lest we have to take our "lessons" all over again.

The Morrigan is also a champion for those who endure abuse, or who have been abused. She teaches how to remain steadfast in the face of the storm, and emerge both a survivor and a victor.

Ravens, black dogs, and crows are sacred to the Morrigan.

The Morrigan's favored colors are black, silver, and red.

Mother Holle. This Germanic goddess, also known as Holle or Hulda, is the caretaker of souls who died as infants or children. She is a wellspring of love and compassion, bringing peace in death and the afterlife. She is also responsible for teaching humanity the art of weaving linen from flax and imparts a knowledge of witchcraft to her followers. Pray to Mother Holle in times of darkness, or in winter when seasonal depression starts to become a problem. She will bring you cheer and hope.

The holly tree, pigeons, and mourning doves are sacred to Mother Holle. Heartfelt and handmade gifts bring her message of love during the holidays.

Mother Holle's favored colors are green, red, white, and silver.

Santa Muerte. This Mexican goddess guides and guards the marginalized, downtrodden, and the struggling. She is a sanctuary for those who work at night or in illicit fields. Despite her skeletal appearance, she is nurturing and uplifting to her followers and is always ready to guard and comfort you in her voluminous cloak. El Dio de Lose Muertos, a public holiday throughout Mexico, is such a resplendent display of light, offerings, and love to this goddess and the beloved dead she protects, that tourists from around the world come to observe it.

Pray to Santa Muerte when you feel as if you have lost all hope, or when you need a miracle. Offer her yellow candles, sweets, and flowers on a Friday, and give her stacks of quarters as payment for her protection.

Santa Muerte favors a range of colors, and each color has a specific meaning depending on the need of the petitioner: yellow or gold for wealth; red for love or family concerns; purple to turn bad situations around and for health issues; black for protection; green for legal issues and for justice; copper to banish negativity; white for purification; amber for good health; blue for insight; and silver for luck and success in life.

Chapter 2 The wiccan deities

In Wicca and different types of Paganism, the Goddess and God incorporate the divine female and male energies of the Universe. For some professionals, inside these energies are endless deities who have existed since before the start of written history.

Gods and goddesses like Osiris and Venus originate before the cutting edge religion of Wicca by a great many years, yet have been recovered over the previous century by the individuals who feel associated with them as a living nearness in their lives. Obviously, like so much else when it comes to Wicca, the manners by which the divine is identified and venerated are very assorted.

DUOTHEISM, POLYTHEISM, OR SOMEWHERE IN BETWEEN?

For some professionals who keep to the conventional duotheistic idea of Wicca, the ancient deities are fused as parts, or "lesser aspects," of the "preeminent" Goddess and God. In this sense, they don't generally have a task to carry out without anyone else. For other people, who will in general fall into the classification of "varied" Wiccans, the consideration of ancient deities might be increasingly polytheistic.

These gods and goddesses may be a piece of custom practice in their own right, notwithstanding the God and Goddess. They might be embraced as "supporter" gods or goddesses, with whom the Witch keeps up a continuous relationship, or they might be respected at specific focuses along the Wheel of the Year. They may need likewise bespoke to for help with magical work, typically with specific sorts of enchantment they are customarily connected with.

It might appear to be odd to some to "get" a divinity from another religion to venerate in a Wiccan setting. In any case, the appropriation of deities from another religion isn't at all another training. Since the commencement of human culture, people have combined and received deities from those they came into contact with, mixing parts of their religion with that of the upgraded one. This could be seen today in Ireland and Latin America, for instance, where agnostic divine beings have been made into Christian holy people. Many Wiccans and different agnostics take the point of view that all deities, and even all religions, originate from a similar unique source.

NEARBY ROOTS AND GLOBAL INFLUENCE

As Wicca advanced over the mid-twentieth century, it eventually came to fuse the personalities of a few deities who had been revered in old times. These regularly came from the religions of the antiquated Egyptian, Greek, Roman, and Celtic civic establishments, yet different deities—especially from the Hindu and Norse pantheons—have likewise turned out to be progressively famous with Wiccans.

Today, Wiccans may work with deities from any pantheon, from anyplace around the world, including Africa, Asia, the Americas, and even the indigenous cultures of Australia and New Zealand. Numerous people work just with deities from their own genetic, social legacy, as a way of connecting with their progenitors from past centuries, while others are attracted to deities with no connection to their own family or ethnic history.

As Wicca has kept on developing, there has been much dialog about "appointment" of deities from existing—and frequently minimized—cultures. Accordingly, a few Wiccans work just with deities from "lost" antiquated religions, for example, that of the Egyptians, Celts, or Norse. Deities from Native America or India may be viewed as an exceed, since they are as yet loved in these cultures today, regardless of whether it's to a lesser degree than it was a couple of hundred years back. Eventually, notwithstanding, these choices are close to home, and, except for those joining a formal coven, up to the person.

making your connections with ancient deities

If you need to investigate the potential outcomes of working with at least one new deities, there are a couple of ways to approach your hunt. You may, as others have done, look into the antiquated culture(s) of the pieces of the world your progenitors originated from. On the other hand, maybe there's a specific area or culture that has always captivated you for reasons unknown you can't exactly put the finger on—if along these lines, start taking a gander at their history, folklore, and deities to perceive what instinctive connections you may find.

You can likewise ask the Goddess and the God to make themselves known to you in the angles that are most proper for your training. This may happen using a fantasy, or some other sign or sign. Numerous Wiccans will say that their deities discovered them, as opposed to the different way, sure to tune in to your internal knowing as you contemplate the subject of who you may connect up within the astral domain.

When an answer winds up obvious, read everything you can on the divinity (or deities) being referred to, so you'll have a more clear feeling of who you're trying to produce an association with. Peruse authentic data about the people and the culture the deities started from, just as the first fantasies they show up in. Get balanced instruction in your deities of decision, as opposed to just receiving the viewpoint of one or a couple of Wiccan specialists. The connection between Wiccans and their deities is strongly close to home and remarkable to every person. The more you think about the divine beings and goddesses you try to work with, the more credible and dumbfounding your connection with them can be.

THE EARTH ELEMENT

The Earth is the establishment of lives, as it is both home and wellspring of sustenance. The Earth Element is ever-present and profoundly flexible, manifesting as both soil and seed, and saw in the unceasing rhythms of development, gather, rot, and recovery.

Earth is spoken to by the various geological highlights discovered everywhere throughout the planet, including woods, fields, caverns, rocks, valleys, and gardens. This "traditional" Element is related to bounty, thriving, and quality.

Not exclusively is Earth the source and sustainer of plant and creature life, yet it has likewise furnished the mud and minerals with which humans have made tools, and the trees and stone we've used to assemble homes and different structures. In any case, Earth's energy has a pernicious side, which might be experienced as earthquakes, torrential slides, or landslides.

The Earth Element can join with water, ingest it, or be cut out by it, contingent upon the measure of every Element, and the equivalent can be said of its association with Fire and Air. In general, Earth is the most "establishing" of the Wiccan Elements, its capacity keeping us quiet and focused amidst life's disorganized wanders.

CONNECTING WITH THE EARTH ELEMENT

Climbing is a perfect way to involve and welcomes all that the Earth brings to the table, regardless of whether you're in the forested areas, on a mountain, or in the desert. In any case, if you don't have simple access to nature save, a pleasant walk around a close-by park works well.

You can likewise basically invest energy in your yard or nursery—indeed, probably the simplest ways to encounter the mending, establishing energies of Earth is to head outside and stand shoeless on the ground. On the other hand, you can rest on the grass, or spot your palm level against the storage compartment of a tree. Notice how your very own energy inconspicuously shifts into a position of more simplicity and stillness when you're physically connecting with the Earth.

If you're a condo occupant without a private outside space, you can at present experience the Element of Earth energies by tending a pruned plant—tenderly contacting the dirt and the leaves and valuing their quality. Cooking is another open door for this connection. For instance, whenever you set up a dinner with root vegetables, first hold the crude, unrinsed potatoes or carrots in your grasp, breathe in their earthy fragrance, and express appreciation for the liberal abundance of the Earth.

PROFOUND AND MAGICAL ASSOCIATIONS OF THE ELEMENT OF EARTH:

Divinity: The Goddess

Energy: ladylike, open

Bearing: North

Tools: Pentacle, a bowl of salt

Hues: green, yellow, dark-colored, dark

Season: Winter

Zodiac Signs: Taurus, Virgo, Capricorn

Enchanted Uses: Salt, an image of Earth, is regularly used to cast the hover before custom. Soil can be added to certain supernatural charms or used to purify gems and different tools. Numerous spells call for covering certain items in the Earth.

THE WATER ELEMENT

Water is regularly thought of as the most basic of the Elements for supporting life. Humans can't live without it, and the equivalent is valid for creatures and vegetation. Before the approach of streets, water furnished humans with the most proficient methods for movement, and it is still hosted to one-fourth of the biodiversity found on Earth. Related with the Moon, clairvoyant capacities, dreams, and the domain of feelings, the Water Element is a shape-shifter, moving effectively all through the world by following the easiest course of action.

It can exist as a strong as ice, or as a gas in modest particles noticeable all around. It appears as puddles after the downpour, to vanish again in the daylight. Water is spoken to by lakes, streams, waterways, seas, and downpour, and is helpful in its purging, purifying, recuperating and sustaining characteristics.

However, it tends to be a risk to life when it manifests as stormy oceans, riptides, and even serious rainstorms. The Water Element is amazing when collaborating with the other traditional Elements, as it can douse Fire, flood the Earth, and join with Air to consume and disintegrate metals. As a rule, water is one of the all the more alleviating Elements when it goes to the human soul.

CONNECTING WITH THE ELEMENT OF WATER

Probably the most pleasant ways to upgrade your vivacious connection with the Element of Water is to go swimming! Common waterways—lakes, streams, lakes, the sea—are perfect, yet pools additionally work well. Pause for a minute to see how you feel previously, during, and after your time in the water, and you'll get a decent feeling of the intensity of this Element. If swimming isn't a choice, wash up or shower, seeing the way the water feels on your skin.

Try valuing the water you drink, expressing gratefulness for its life-supporting properties. Go for a stroll in the downpour, or tune in to its sound falling outside your window. You can likewise play chronicles of sea waves, foaming rivers, or rainstorms to get the substance of water streaming in your life. At long last, absorbing a custom shower before observing Sabbats and Esbats, or before mysterious work always upgrades your capacity.

SPIRITUAL AND MAGICAL INSTITUTION OF ELEMENT OF WATER:

God: the Goddess

Energy: open, female

Direction: West

Apparatuses: cup, cauldron

Colors: blue, green, indigo, dark

Season: Autumn

Zodiac Signs: Pisces, Cancer, Scorpio

Magical uses: In a dark bowl, water can be utilized for scrying. Water is a base element for most magical teas and mixtures and is used in different forms of spellwork.

THE FIRE ELEMENT

Fire is maybe the most hypnotizing of the Wiccan Elements, but then it's the one in particular that can't be contacted without damage to the body. While not vital for human survival—we did live without it for a short early period in long history—the Fire Element is positively essential to a solid and agreeable presence. For more than 100,00 years, Fire has made it feasible for us to prepare nutritious suppers, work and play after nightfall, and warm ourselves in colder atmospheres.

Spoken to by the Sun and its light, just as the stars, deserts, and volcanoes, Fire is the element of transformation, and is related with enlightenment, wellbeing, quality, and inventiveness. Continuously moving, notwithstanding when established in one spot, it is the most dynamic and vivified of the traditional Elements. As a commitment to the normal request of the Earth,

Fire keeps backwoods sound through cycles of consuming and recovery.

This equivalent power is likewise risky and fatal when unchecked, which is why this Element directions such as regard from the individuals who try to utilize it. Any of different Elements can douse the fire, yet it is likewise the main Element that must have another substance to expend to keep up its reality.

INTERFACING WITH THE FIRE ELEMENT

Most would concur that the most charming approach to appreciate the Element of Fire is in the outside at a joyful bonfire, either alone or with companions and friends and family. Many covens perform their ritual work outside around a fire when conceivable. Tuning in to the snap of the fuel as it consumes and viewing the coals discharge sparkles into the air can instigate a quiet, thoughtful state.

The equivalent is valid for looking at a light fire if you're hoping to interface with the Fire Element on a littler scale. Moreover, flares and smoke from any Fire source can be "read" for dreams and signs, because of the developments and shapes that they make, and a few traditions utilize the fiery remains from ritual fires for divination. Notwithstanding, a genuine fire isn't carefully important for communing with this Element.

Investing energy under the Sun is another method for interfacing, for, although the Sun is formed from gas, its warmth can surely be blazing. You can likewise emblematically respect the Element of Fire by taking part in vivacious exercise or ritual move, which raises the warmth of your body, stirring your inner Fire.

SPIRITUAL AND MAGICAL ASSOCIATIONS OF THE ELEMENT OF FIRE:

Divinity: God

Energy: manly, projective

Direction: South

Instruments: wand or athame, contingent upon tradition; candles

Colors: red, gold, red, orange, white

Season: Summer

Zodiac Signs: Aries, Leo, Sagittarius

Magical Uses: Candles are utilized both as subordinates to enchantment, to improve the air for spellwork, and as the essential focal point of flame spells. Fire is likewise utilized in consuming spells.

THE AIR ELEMENT

Essential to the moment by-minute presence, Air is the ever-present Element that is surrounding us, yet difficult to see. Without a doubt, it is just obvious through the cooperations it has with different Elements: Earth, Water, and Fire. The Air Element is spoken to by the sky, wind, feathered creatures, and peaks, and is related with the psyche, the acumen, correspondence, and divination.

Like Water, Air is an Element of development. It isn't fixed to the ground, however, rather can ascend and go far and wide. Air's energies can cause quick change, for example, shifts in the wind's direction and variances in temperature. Air is basic to life because it contains oxygen, yet additionally because it dissipates seeds over the ground with the goal that new vegetation can flourish in the Earth.

The damaging characteristics of Air come as tempests—particularly tornadoes—just as perilously cold or hot temperatures. When adequately vivacious, Air can move Water and quench Fire. Air can both move Earth—through blowing soil—and be impeded by it, for example, when the safe house of a cavern obstructs the wind. As a delicate breeze, be that as it may, Air can be experienced as the delicate, consoling murmur of the God and Goddess.

INTERFACING WITH THE AIR ELEMENT

We are genuinely in consistent connection with Air as we are continually relaxing. Be that as it may, being aware of your breath is significant when it comes to identifying with this "old style" Element. A wide range of breathing activities, for example, those found in yoga and contemplation rehearses, can enable you to upgrade your spiritual association with Air. So can going for a stroll in the lively wind, seeing how the air moves over your skin.

Try investing energy outside in the natural air whenever you can. Value each cool wind you experience on a hot day. Watch the developments of mists and trees as they influence in the wind. If you're longing for a more profound association with Air however can't get outside, turn on a fan and sit directly before it, expressing gratefulness for its cool, reviving embodiment.

SPIRITUAL AND MAGICAL ASSOCIATIONS OF THE ELEMENT OF AIR:

Divinity: God

Energy: manly, projective

Direction: East

Devices: wand or athame, contingent upon tradition; incense; ringer

Colors: yellow, white, silver

Season: Spring

Zodiac Signs: Gemini, Libra, Aquarius

Magical Uses: Air is associated with the consuming of incense and in smirching rituals. Breath-work and ritual developments and move likewise use the energy of Air. The direction of the wind can be utilized to improve specific kinds of spellwork.

THE SPIRIT ELEMENT—THE FIFTH ELEMENT (AKASHA)

While the four "old-style" Elements—Earth, Air, Fire, and Water—together involve the physical world, there is the Fifth Element, regularly alluded to as Spirit, that exists inside each of the four. The Spirit Element is irrelevant, yet present no matter what, and doesn't exist separated from whatever else. It is undetectable, yet fundamental for association and harmony between every single other Element.

Spirit is what is called forward in ritual, through the summoning of the God and Goddess, and the Elements. It abides in us as living creatures, both when we know about it and when we are most certainly not. In any case, when we know about Spirit, and when we have clear and centered expectations, we can use this center, basic energy to manifest wanted change through magical work.

A UNIVERSAL ENERGY

Spirit is not normal for the other four Elements in that, since it is a piece of everything, it doesn't have a specific ritual or magical correspondences (in any event in many traditions). One exemption is color—it might be spoken to by the color white, as white is involved all colors joined. Spirit doesn't have a related sexual orientation, energy type, season, or cardinal direction. It is associated with the whole Wheel of the Year and every magical device.

Spirit is extremely the Element of heavenly knowledge, which needs no specific images to be perceived. In any case, when talking about the Wiccan Elements, the pentacle is frequently referenced, since the star has five—one for every Element—and is encompassed by a circle, which can symbolize how Spirit holds all of creation together.

THE SPIRIT ELEMENT: NAMING THE UN-NAMEABLE

In old Greece, where the Western concept of the Elements begins, it wound up evident to Aristotle and others that something was absent from the old style set of physical substances—Earth, Air, Fire, and Water. The Greeks were not exacting realists—they perceived an awesome nearness and revered numerous individual divinities, so they realized that there was more to the Universe than meets the eye. The word "Aether" was connected to what the Greek logicians saw as the "upper air," or the air that the gods took in the heavenly circle. It had at first been viewed as a significant aspect of the Element of Air, and however, later it turned out to be certain that this energy was an Element in its own right. Today, numerous Wiccan traditions utilize the word "Aether" as the name of the Fifth Element.

Others, notwithstanding, allude to the Spirit Element as Akasha, a Sanskrit word generally deciphering as "space" or "environment." This isn't implied in the cutting edge feeling of "space," yet rather a nonattendance of physical form, an energy that is available no matter what yet isn't physical itself. Akasha is viewed as the "first" Element, from which all creation came. This Eastern concept isn't indistinguishable from the Western concept of "spirit," however the similitudes were adequate for later spiritual and religious traditions to embrace "Akasha" into their phrasings.

Regardless of which term is utilized, the Element of Spirit—the Fifth Element—can be tricky to get a handle on, although it is inside and surrounding us. It very well may be especially difficult to keep in mindfulness in the occupied, boisterous present-day world we live in. That is why contemplation, supplication, and ritual are cherished practices among spiritual searchers of various types. When we get calm and still, when we go to the special raised area and watch the consecrated rituals, we can all the more effectively get back in contact with this widely inclusive Element—an energy that is so elusive and baffling, it's no big surprise that it has such a significant number of different names.

Chapter 3 Wicca in our modern world

With the creation of various rituals — whether they were for fertility, for growing crops, for success in hunting or for better weather conditions — there arose a necessity for someone to conduct the rituals. This individual would be well-versed about the beliefs, deities, and requirements of the tribes.

These individuals were thought to bring better results when conducting rituals.

Dr. Murray had the belief that in many areas of Europe, these priests became widely known as the "Wise Ones" or Wicca.

Although this statement is often debated (not the fact there were priests who were called Wicca but about how widespread the name Wicca was initially), what is known is that in many Anglo-Saxon kingdoms, kings and rulers would not make important decisions without consulting with the Witan (derived from the name Wiccan, used to refer to a single wise person where Wicca denoted a whole group of people).

The Witan were labelled the "Council of Wise Ones."

Eventually, the level of importance of the Wicca began to rise. These priests had to have thorough knowledge of not just magick, lore, and divination, but also of history, medicine, and politics.

They were not just priests, but close advisors to the king. In other words, a mere whisper of suggestion into the ears of kings could send two factions into a state of war. Indeed, priests began to hold considerable power.

To the general public, the Wicca were the mouthpieces of the gods. But when it came to performing rituals, the same Wicca were considered as equals to gods.

Then Christianity arrived.

The Growth of Christianity

Many people believe that Christianity involved a mass conversion but that was not the case. In fact, during its early stages, Christians came under heavy persecution. Both Jewish and Roman leaders targeted Christianity for numerous reasons.

After a great fire broke out in Rome in the year 64 A.D., the emperor Nero came under heavy criticism. He needed to shift the focus of attention away from himself or risk being deposed (or backstabbed by someone you know. It was Rome after all).

He found the perfect scapegoat in Christianity. What made his campaign of targeting the young religion even more successful was the fact that back then people already harbored a misconception about Christianity. Many Christian rituals were thought to include acts of cannibalism. Others were considered to encourage incest.

The stage was practically set for anyone who wanted to blame Christianity for some calamity like, say, a great fire. Through such events, Christianity had a slow growth, but it still found a way to spread vastly.

Eventually, an attempt was made by Pope Gregory the Great to mass convert people. To make this happen, he made the people build churches in the same spot that older temples and places of worship were established. It was as though the old religions were being removed and overthrown by Christianity.

However, the pope did not exactly receive the results that he wanted. You see, people were not as gullible or as open-minded to the presence of a new religion as he had hoped. During the time of the construction of the first Christian church, the only stonemasons, artisans, and labor available were people who were "pagans," a term referring to anyone who practiced a religion that was not Christianity. While decorating the churches, these pagan workers added symbols and designs of their own religion into the structure. These little additions were done cleverly, in a manner that would escape the scrutiny of Christian priests.

But since Christianity was slowly growing, Wicca and other pagan religions were its opposition. There are, of course, many ways to get rid of opposition. You could sit down and have a proper conversation. You could discuss various logical steps that each party can take to ensure the harmonious existence of both entities.

Or you could do what the Christians did: turn the belief systems of the opposition into something nefarious and sinister.

The church focused its efforts on shifting the perspective of the people about the so called "Old Religions" (a.k.a. Wicca and other pagan beliefs). Their main focus was to show that these Old Religions worshipped the devil. Hence, the very image of the Horned god was adopted into Christianity as a symbol of the Devil. Lo and behold! A devil with horns was born (or created, depending on how you look at it).

When the idea of the Devil became rooted in the practices, a singular, most obvious conclusion was drawn: paganism involved devil worshipping! Eventually, this idea of the Devil and paganism became a staple of the religion. As the belief endured, so did its ability to permeate into every section of society.

In fact, if you were to count the number of movies that showed witches as people who are conjuring demonic presences, haunting the woods (come on, we have "The Blair Witch Project" and its many sequels to prove that), or simply creating mischief to unsuspecting humans and compare that to those movies that show witches as people living in the woods, then you might notice the difference.

In fact, many missionaries and priests in parts of the world have used the rhetoric about pagan worshippers and the Devil.

But I digress. Back to the Horned god.

In those days, during the growth of Christianity, it did not matter what kind of people followed Wicca or whether they lived much happier and fulfilled lives than Christians. As long as they were practicing a faith that did not include Jesus, they were shunned from society or were asked (asked being a polite term) to convert.

The Devil Wears Nada

According to Professor Henry Ansgar Kelly of the University of California, Los Angeles (Biography.com Editors, 2014), the Devil is mentioned just three times in the Old Testament. Even during those appearances, the Devil performs actions that are actually administered by God. That doesn't seem like the evil king of hell that we all know about.

Here is another fact to consider.

The whole idea of "evil" being attributed to the Devil is a result of a mistranslation. In the original Hebrew version of the Old Testament, the word for devil was Ha-satan and in the original Greek version of the New Testament, the word used was Diabolos, both words meaning "adversary" or "opponent." There was never any separation of powers when it came to dealing with religion.

Because there was an all-loving and all-good God, there was just the need to create an entity to give the people the idea that their misdeeds are not going to go overlooked. After all, if God decided to suddenly toss people into eternal fires or make them carry boulders forever, then it doesn't sound like the actions of an "all-good and all-forgiving" entity. They needed another manager for that department.

Even the views of monotheism (the idea that there exists only one God) was not actually developed by Christianity, Judaism, Islam or any of the religions that we are familiar with. In fact, it was an idea born in Ancient Egypt, during the reign of Akhanaten.

The goat was a symbol of the Horned god. Nowadays, anything connected to the Devil or dark arts use the goat as a symbol.

Begone Heathens!

As Christianity grew, the Old Religions began to fade away slowly. Much of the practice of Wicca was conducted in the outskirts of the countries. There were very few people who would actually openly declare themselves as part of the Wicca belief.

The words "pagan" and "heathen" were then used to describe anyone who practiced the Old Religion, which is not a bad thing actually.

Surprised? I bet you are thinking that I just went over the edge, that I am about to tell everyone how terrible Wicca is.

Not even close.

You see, the word "pagan" is derived from the Latin word "pagani," which translates to "people who live in the country." Essentially, it was used to refer to Wiccans, Witches and anyone who practiced the Old Religion.

Additionally, the word "heathen" is also Latin, translating to "one who dwells on heath." Heath is a word that describes an open and uncultivated land. Some define it as an area that resembles a countryside. The terms were more descriptive of the nature of non-Christians when they were first used. All ideas of the two words being derogatory are a modern construct and quite incorrect.

Chapter 4 Wicca and Satanism

Although there is plenty of information regarding what it means to be Wiccan, a few people still believe that Wicca is closely associated with Satanism. However, these two have no relation to each other. The relationship between the two is a very old confused notion.

A fundamental explanation that can explain the relationship between Wicca and Satanism is the fact that the two do not believe in the idea of "God" as is perceived by Christians. Since the witch-hunting times, there have been people who, because they do not understand Wicca, simply mark it as being wrong and satanic because it falls outside of their narrow beliefs. According to their ideas, any individual that does not agree with specific religious beliefs must then be "allied with the devil." Unfortunately, this notion still continues today despite several advancements in tradition.

The mystery of Wicca has been influenced by some aspects in history. Gerald Gardner who is believed to be the founder of Wicca was interested in Aleister Crowley's work when they met in the mid-20th century. A couple of traditions and beliefs in Gardner's first coven were greatly influenced by Crowley and were later taught by Gardner.

During his time, Aleister Crowley was highly influential in Witchcraft circles. As mentioned earlier, he was the originator of the spelling "Magick." He was a great writer who drew inspiration from different beliefs and traditions as well as secret groups around the world. Crowley's work drew controversy on what was considered to be "sinister" symbolism. When asked, he often denied being a Satanist and seemingly so, there existed no proof to demonstrate that he worshipped a figure called "Satan." Crowley did not care to explain himself nor did he bother to clearly distance himself from Satanism. The relationship between Gardner and Crowley was enough to speculate Wicca to be related to Satanism because Crowley never mentioned being in Gardner's coven or being a witch.

In order to understand the difference that exists between Wicca and Satanism, it might be helpful to discuss the origin of Satan and Satanism. According to Christianity, Satan is a "fallen angel" who was chased from Heaven and now lives in Hell, who works to ensure that individuals are enticed to sin so that they end up with him in Hell when they die instead of going to God in Heaven.

In Judaism, where Christianity gets its founding principles, "Satan" was perceived very differently. In Hebrew, "Satan" means "hinderer" and was seen as a part of God whose work it was to test individuals with the aim of making them a better individual. There can be no existence of good if there is no bad. This then means that Satan was really just working for God.

It is important to understand that in Wicca "Satan" does not exist and therefore Wiccans are not worshipping him at all. Claiming so will mean therefore that Muslims should get blamed for worshipping Brighid the Celtic goddess or that Buddhists revere the divinity of antiquated Aztecs.

There are agnostic gatherings and religious people who define themselves as "Satanists." Satanists hold insights and perspectives that they believe in. Some of these individuals consider themselves to be responding against Christianity and its narrow-minded beliefs while others believe that Satan is a kind being. Satanists do not essentially practice wicked acts and hurt others although there are some who actually do so. Their belief system states that it is individuals and not spirits who are in control of their lives.

Notably, any magic practiced by Wiccans is guided by "The Wiccan Rede" which essentially means that no Wiccan practice serves to harm anybody.

The magic carried out during Esbats and Sabbats utilizes ritual tools such as candles, herbs and crystals. Just like magic, these rituals have the practitioners using affirmations and chants that reach out to God and the Goddess as well as other deities to impact an outcome. Wiccan magic does not intend to cause harm whether intentionally or unintentionally because Wiccan traditions seek to live in harmony with the Earth. The result of magic should only work to benefit its recipients as well as practitioners.

A council of American Witches gathered in 1973 where over 70 Wiccan were in attendance. The 70 Wiccan came from different Wiccan subsets and, as a unit, they worked together to develop the 13 core principles. This set of principles were later recognized by most Wiccans then living in the United States. These principles are still respected to date.

Although Wicca is truly fluid and not holding onto any staunch or strict rules, there are two key rules that most Wiccans who practice communally or alone adhere to. The two key rules are the following:

1)   The Wiccan Rede

The Wiccan Rede was originally a 26-line poem. It is a statement of moral guidelines that govern Wiccans. The statement simply means that one should not harm others in their practice. This is translated to be the "golden rule." The Wiccan Rede states, "That it harm none, do as thou wilt."

2)   The Wiccan three-fold law

The rule states that whatever one does, the results are in three-fold. This means any act, whether spiritual or not. This law is also referred to as the law of Karma.

If you have ever wondered whether Wiccans are Witches or if Wiccans are Witches, rest assured that many others wonder the same thing too. There are Wiccans who consider themselves Witches and there are others who do not. In the same way, there are individuals who practice Witchcraft but do not recognize themselves as Wiccans. The confusion between these two terms is understood because in the past the two have been used interchangeably as well as on numerous occasions in the same context.

The Wiccans who do not recognize themselves as Witches simply do not practice magic, which is considered to be what most refer to as "Black Magic." These Wiccans mark the turning of the Wheel of the Year, worship the God and the Goddess and live in harmony with nature. However, they do not work to impact the energies at work in the universe to realize desired outcomes in their lives. Therefore, these Wiccans are truly not Witches.

Notably so, what we currently call Wicca was previously considered to be Witchcraft. This was practiced by Gardner among other people dating back to early 1940s all through to 1960s when Gardnerian and Alexandrian Wicca traditions were conceptualized and practiced. These pioneers of contemporary Witchcraft recognized themselves as Witches long before the term "Wicca" was conceptualized. The term "Wicca" only came into existence when the practice spread to the United States. Wicca is therefore not connected to the type of Craft that is modern day Witchcraft.

The term "Wicca" actually originates from an Old English word which means "alchemist." With the advancement of the English dialect, "Wicca" transitioned into "Witch" an etymological occurrence in the 1500s. In the Old English dialect, "Wiccan" was the plural of "Wicca" while today "Wiccan" means the practitioners of "Wicca." Gardner called his coven members "Wicca" an aspect that is said to be the origin of Wicca.

A great number of Witches comment about their aim to recover the sanctity of the name witch from Christian mistreatment of the word when the name "witch" was not a respected title but an allegation. During that period, nobody would openly recognize themselves as a witch. Happily, that is not the case today. There is still plenty of work to be done to dignify the name "Witch" because it still holds implications of an evil witch or angry women. It could be for these reasons that a number of Wiccans choose to not recognize themselves as Witches.

Having a Book of Shadows is therefore not a requirement for being Wiccan. It is, however, an important tool for a number of reasons. It is a record of one's data or experiences. A number of Wiccans have a number of books that contain rituals, ceremonies and magic spells. You may read from it during rituals as opposed to trying to learn everything at once. In your practice, you can identify in the Book of Shadows what you use the most. You may also record in it your successful spells among other experiences you would like to record during your practice.

To make your own Book of Shadows as a solitary practitioner, you are at liberty to decide how your Book of Shadows will look. Some use a black covered book, others an extravagant diary while others use an electronic gadget and go ahead to share their book online.

One down to Earth suggestion, in case you're the out-dated sort who still uses ink and paper, is to think about holding off on including new material until you're certain of it. For instance, you should need to record a specific spell or new custom succession on isolated paper first and give it a shot before submitting it to your Book of Shadows. In any case, regardless of how you approach it, realize that you can't miss the point. It's your adventure, and the Book of Shadows is your movement log, which you can keep on adding to, subtracting from, and alter as you feel it merits it. However, if you place thoughts onto paper, you won't need to keep making alterations to your book, which will give it more substance to readers.

Magic is about energy—your own energy, the energy of the Universe, the energy of the divinities, elementals, guides, and other non-physical elements you may work with, and the energy of the aim you're doing something amazing for. It follows, at that point, that the energy of the physical apparatuses you work with is a critical factor in the achievement of your magic, just as the nature of any customs and ceremonies you execute as a component of your Wiccan practice. Thus, it's vital to cleanse new ceremonial instruments and spell elements of any undesirable leftover energy, and after that to charge them with deliberate, positive energy before utilizing them in custom or spell work.

Undesirable energy can come from a wide range of actions or places and that's why all new equipment needs to go through a cleansing process. You have to take into account that anyone touching the items used for magic can affect the energy of that item in a negative way. On the off chance that you buy something used, there's a significantly more grounded energy present in that thing, from its past owner(s). Have you at any point bought something at a thrift store and felt your state of mind change as you held it? That is another person's leftover energy!

It is vital that you clear all negative energy from anything that you use within a ceremony, which is why preparation is essential. It is merely a case of removing the negative energy just as you may clean up the dust from a piece of furniture. In any case, the cleansing step is an imperative one so that your spells will be more effectively influenced by your own energies, rather than that of previous owners.

So how would you clear undesirable energy? There are a few distinct strategies, and some are more qualified for specific things than others. For instance, ocean salt is a good choice because of its density, especially with regards to cleansing precious stones and candles. It works by retention—simply cover the thing in a bowl of salt and leave it for a few hours to a day and then get rid of the salt. (Make sure to discard the salt in a place where it is kept away from your apparatus.) A minor departure from this strategy is to break up ocean salt in water and drench or sprinkle your items. Be that as it may, contingent upon their specific structure, not all things hold up well in a salt shower so do research and make sure that the item being cleansed will not suffer detrimental effects from contact with salt.

Daylight is another way of cleansing negative or unwanted energy. Spread your ceremonial apparatus out in direct daylight for no less than one hour and any undesirable energy will be consumed with extreme heat, leaving them clean and prepared to be filled with your very own energy, which is vital. Evening sun works a similar way and is best for any things that may be damaged by the light and warmth from the Sun. This is particularly relevant to specific gems and herbs you might need to use in spell work. The evening sun is less harsh.

Smirching with sage, rosemary, lavender, as well as other purifying herbs is an old tradition practiced by shamanic groups far and wide. It attempts to get rid of undesirable energy from items, physical spaces, and even individuals. Sound is another phenomenal method to separate and scatter stale energy—have a go at ringing a bell over your increasingly fragile ceremonial apparatus and this will help to get rid of negative energy and make them ready for your use.

The next stage in setting up your ceremonial devices for spell work is filling them with your own energy ready for use. For instance, you may fill a citrine precious stone with upbeat, sure energy with the goal that this vibration will be accessible to you at whatever point you need to touch it or hold the stone. In case you're charging a flame for a particular spell, you'll center the energy upon the association between the light and the objective you're attempting to achieve.

Both daylight and twilight can be used as to charge your equipment with positive energy, so you can basically clear bad energy and prepare that equipment with your own energy. Simply make sure, in case you're charging it for a particular objective, that you center the cleansing process on your intended use of that object. Another straightforward strategy is to lay your item on a pentacle piece (which has just been cleared and charged). For an additional "support," lay the pentacle in daylight or evening sunlight. Amethyst and quartz gems are likewise fantastic chargers in their own right, so you can put herbs, little stones, custom adornments or whatever other items will fit right onto these shimmering wonders.

Regardless of which strategy you use, the energy of your own engaged aim is the way to succeed in the procedure. Picture the result you're looking for when you charge your ceremonial instruments ready for magic. Material association—grasping the item or putting your fingers on it while it lays on a surface—is a decent method to exchange your energy to it. Using expressions of aim can truly enable you to sharpen your focus, so think of a few words that express your desires here. For instance, while charging for a particular spell, you may state:

"I charge this [name the object]

through the Universal power

to bring [name the enchanted purpose]

into my life.

So leave it alone."

With regards to ceremonial instruments, for example, your wand or athame, this cleansing is commonly consolidated by what we call "sanctification." Consecration, for the most part, includes evoking the God and Goddess as well as the Elements as a method for associating the ceremonial items with your specific intent. Contingent upon how you approach your training, this may be a more intricate process than that used for creating spells. Regularly, individuals will are able to create a vacuum of energy by stating the specific purpose of this cleansing. They may even make an altar upon which to place items. Special stepped areas are generally blessed on a pentacle, or a pentacle may be drawn with a wand or athame over the article in the focal point of the raised area. In case you're new to the Wiccan practice, you should try a couple of ways to deal with cleansing and energizing your equipment and will eventually settle upon one particular method that works for you.

You may find at first that you have difficulty in clearing out the negative energy of items you intend to use. In any case, be consistent with your practice, because this is an important part of preparing yourself. You will notice that things change when the energy of the items is positively charged and the item has taken on your energy because your spells will become more successful and you will feel the energy from the items used will be more powerful. If you don't believe in the importance of this cleansing, try to cast a spell with an item that has not been cleansed and you will soon learn the difference because the energy going into the spell will be negatively charged and the spell unlikely to work.

Many new Wiccans wonder if there is a dress code for Wiccans and wonder what they should wear. They also question whether they should be clothed or naked. While the facts demonstrate that the first Gardnerian types of Witchcraft included customary nakedness and numerous conventional covens still pursue this training, skyclad is positively by all account, not the only alternative. Truth be told, today there are numerous inventive, diverse ways to deal with Wiccan dress and adornments, as you will see below.

In case you're looking to join a coven or a casual Wiccan circle, you'll need to discover what their conventions are as far as custom clothing is concerned (assuming any clothing policy has been adopted) and pick clothing that you're okay with. Obviously, in case you're a solo Wiccan practitioner, you don't have to check with anybody but yourself with regard to what you wear. In the event where you pursue a convention that calls for working skyclad on your own and you're alright with it, by all means do! For those who are not aware of it, sky-clad means naked and it is believed by Pagans that wearing clothing actually takes away some of the positivity of connection between themselves and nature, and thus that clothes get in the way.

Ceremonial robes are regularly worn by Wiccans and different Pagans as a method of isolating themselves from the ordinary everyday parts of life and improving their feeling of magic and secrets. For these professionals, wearing a robe is important and plays a part in how effectively they follow their craft. These robes are usually made from fabrics that are natural. Commonly Wiccans wear nothing underneath their ceremonial robes. However, this is an individual decision—as usual, and you must do what's right for you.

Robes can be bought or you can make them yourself. You can discover extremely straightforward examples online so that regardless of how talented you are at sewing, you can usually find what you are looking for. Regardless of whether you're purchasing or sewing the gown yourself, make certain that you focus on a very essential element: combustibility. There are some exceptionally pretty robes that are not at all practical, especially if you are working with flames, so this part of the choice is very important. Man-made fabrics are usually not a good choice.

A few specialists like to wear a shroud because of following old customs, especially if a ceremony is being held outside. These can be worn over ceremonial robes or ordinary apparel, yet are commonly not worn individually since they generally just attach at the neckline. Likewise, with robes, you can discover a lot of pre-made shrouds on the web, or make your own. You could likewise do some chasing around at vintage shops and repurpose an old article of clothing into your own custom shroud! In any case, looking online will give you an idea as to the necessary clothing for your craft, and it's up to you to make that individual choice.

There's no need to make or buy exceptional Wiccan garments for your work if you're a solo practitioner. A lot of Wiccans basically wear their normal clothes, or clothes that allow them to think with positive vibes rather than those that are constrictive and bring out any kind of negativity. Thus, a floral dress or something you feel good about will suffice.

Although there is no rule about this, many Wiccans will wear at least one piece of enchanted jewelry to help them with their spells or to give them the extra positive energy needed to perform them. This may be something like a pentacle or otherworldly image made into a locket and worn close to the heart. Rings are used occasionally or even wristbands or anklets. Some Wiccans even used a pearl encrusted headpiece. The important thing is that whatever you add to your person should improve your own energy so that you are more effective in your craft.

If you do not feel that something is adding extra energy, then try to change it until you find something that gives off that positive vibration that you are seeking.

As with all paraphernalia pertaining to Wiccan craft, all objects that are worn on the person should also be cleansed of their negative energy before being charged with your energy. That's a very important part of preparation.

Regardless of the suggestions made, you need to be aware that apparel is not as important as the energy that you emit. Therefore, be aware that ill-fitting clothing will not help your cause and that it would be better to dress in things that add to your positive vibration, rather than things that hinder you.

If you are working in conjunction with a coven, then of course, your apparel should be in line with that coven and it's worth taking advice from experienced Wiccans within that group. However, if you are practicing alone, that doesn't apply and you should recognize that your powerful energies come from inside of you, rather than through the clothing that you choose, but that this energy does need to flow so that suitable apparel will allow it to do so.

Wicca is all about you and nature. The elements that you introduce into the practice are a personal choice. The way that you feel within yourself is a powerful force. If you feel that your energy will be increased by changing into the role of Wiccan when working on your Wiccan craft, then this is your choice. If, however, you feel false energy when wearing clothing you have tried, then perhaps the clothing chosen is not the best for practicing your craft.

Chapter 5 The Campaign Against Witches

It was not a good time for anyone to believe in anything that did not conform with the ideas of Christianity. There was a spread of an anti-witch smear campaign, mostly propagated by the churches. It did not help that Witches and Wiccans did not practice their religion openly, creating an air of mysticism around them. Additionally, the fact that they included rituals that did not involve just singing hymns and praising the Lord turned them into outcasts.

Everything that the Witches did was used against them.

Witches used to perform rituals of magick to promote fertility and improve crop conditions. The church claimed that it was because of these rituals that women became barren and that crops were not healthy. There was no mention of the idea that if Witches were indeed responsible for the actions they were accused of, then everyone would suffer equally. Anyone who raised the point was silenced immediately under threat of persecution.

One of the rituals performed by the Witches to improve fertility involved participants to head out to the fields during a full moon. They would then use long tools such as poles, pitchforks, and broomsticks and ride these tools like riding toy horses. They would circle the field and chant, asking the gods to grow the crops with much health. The followers would leap as high as possible into the air. The higher they jumped, the taller they wanted the crops to grow. This was a form of sympathetic magick that did not have the most noble of intentions, but a harmless ritual.

To the church; however, this was an opportunity to turn the idea of Witchcraft on itself. According to the church, the Witches were working against the crops in an effort to destroy them. They were not leaping into the air, but rather flying on broomsticks and other tools. Surely such actions could only mean that these people were under the influence of the Devil!

Soon, the fear of Witches took hold among the masses. In 1484, Pope Innocent VIII used this fear to persecute Witches openly. It was two years later that two monks, Heinrich (Institoris) Kramer and Jakob Sprenger, wrote a book that dealt with anti-witchery.

The book was named **Malleus Maleficarum**, which translates to The Witch Hammer. Using the acts of Witches to brand them as evil, the book included detailed instructions on how to deal with Witches. At that time, the official censor (an official or a group of officials responsible for looking at works of art and declaring them as too obscene, politically motivated or a harm to society) was the University of Cologne. Upon reading the book, most of the professors decided that they did not want to be involved with the book at all.

Kramer and Sprenger on the other hand decided to use more nefarious actions to get the approval on the book. They forged an approval letter from the university, which essentially said that the work of **Malleus Maleficarum** was approved and even admired by many of the professors.

The result was like bringing a match to a flammable substance. There was mass panic and hysteria. People took to the streets to condemn Witches. Anyone who was even remotely suspected of being involved in rituals was brought to the streets or were turned over to the authorities. A sense of religious fervor and hatred against Witches took form, one that was not based on any rational thinking. This mood spread all over Europe.

For the next 300 years, Witches would be persecuted. No matter what violence was inflicted on Witches, it was deemed acceptable by the church on grounds of "removing evil." In some cases, inhabitants of an entire village were put to death because of the presence of just one or two Witches among them.

In 1586, the Archbishop of Treveres had concluded that the local Witches had caused a severe change in the weather, turning it into a freezing winter. By using methods of torture, a "confession" was obtained, which led to the rounding up of more than a hundred men and women. These men and women were then burned to death.

As we had seen, fertility was an important part of Witchcraft. For this reason, there were certain sexual rites that were also enacted by Wiccan. When the Wiccans were brought in front of Christian churches, they were asked to recount these rites in detail, much to the delight and amusement of the judges and members of the court.

In the end, there was never an exact number to account for the people who were hanged, burned, or tortured by the church. But many estimates say that the total number is close to nine million people. Remember that not all of the people who were sent to their deaths were Witches. As the Witch trials spread across the region, it gave opportunities for people to get rid of anyone they harbored a grudge against or simply disliked.

In fact, a good example of how innocent people were caught in the persecution can be understood from the famous case of the Witches of Salem, Massachusetts. It was never confirmed whether any of the victims who were put to their death were followers of witchcraft or the Old Religion. In fact, many people were outstanding members of the community and even the local church!

God and Goddess

Wiccans worship their gods and goddesses through critical awareness. They are aware of the following:

- There is only one "source".
- All gods and goddesses represent a variety of faces from the source.
- All living things on Earth are elements of the source.

The Wiccans' deepest loyalty is to their gods and goddesses which is the "one" behind the mask. The one is the thing you form all your devotion to. The most important thing in Wicca is that you **do** worship your gods and goddesses. The first rule in Wicca and the way of your life is in devoting and dedicating all your actions and your awareness to the creator - whatever that may be for you.

In any religion, they all have one thing in common which is to worship their one divine source. In Christianity, it is a higher power, and in Hinduism, they have many gods. In China, they worship the Jade Emperor.

The gods and goddesses are the ones who share their lives with you and with whom you choose to share your journey. In Wicca, the deity is a transformational spiritual practice to perceive the divine as something that lives in every being as every being:

- Your Mother - the Goddess
- Your brother - The God
- Your baby - The Divine
- Your friend - The Source
- Your enemy - The One
- Your cat/pet - All that is
- Your self - The Eternal Light

The list explains that everything around you is your gods and goddesses. When you truly understand that the divinity is none above others is when you can fully begin to worship all that surrounds you. The list above is what the Wiccan deities are.

The Wiccan holidays of the Wheel of the Year

Wiccans have what is called the "Wheel of the Year", and it is used to mark down all the major solar and lunar events, which are what their holidays are based on. For example, the Sabbats are for celebrating the sun's influence on Earth, which is the seasonal growing cycle. Wiccan Esbats celebrate the moon phases, especially the full moon.

Here is a list of the Wiccan Wheel Year:

Name	Holiday	Earth Event	Date	Occasion
Samhain	Halloween	fifteen' Scorpio	October 31st	Cleansing and releasing. Celebrating the dead. The Pagan new year.
Yule	Christmas	Winter Solstice	December 22nd	Rebirth.
Bridgid	Candlemas	fifteen' Aquarius	February 2nd	Purification, allegiance, and initiation

Eostara	Easter	Spring Equinox	March 21st	Innovation, revitalization, and new beginnings.
Beltane	May Day	fifteen' Taurus	May 1st	Fertility, happiness, and passion that fuels life.
Lithia		Summer Solstice	June 21st	Passage, and planning
Lammas	First Harvest	fifteen' Leo	August 1st	Appreciation, abundance, and fruition.
Mabon	Thanksgiving	Autumn Equinox	September 21st	Giving thanks, thoughtfulness, and expression.

On all these holidays and events, it is essential for the Wiccan to do traditional rituals. Whether you do it in a group setting, in a quiet get-together, or a full-on drama ritual routine, the point is that you do worship and do the ritual. The rituals consist of:

- Honoring the divine in all the elements of life
- Recharging or regenerate your spiritual batteries
- Centering and balancing yourself with Earth's shifting energies.

The Wiccan dates are confusing, but to start a holiday or a "new day", the Wiccan dates start on the previous day at dusk once the sun has gone down. Each coven or witch will have their own way of doing things, but most of the time, the holiday starts at sunrise on the date.

Chapter 6 Sabbats and Esbats

Sabbats and Esbats are the time for regrowth, birth, or death of something. They are old traditions that have gone on for centuries, and thanks to our ancestors, they are the start of how our world works today. There are eight main Sabbats revolving around the sun; The Wheel of the Year starts like this:

Yule (Winter Solstice)

On December 21st, 22nd, or 23rd, "Yule" - the winter solstice - starts. Normal people would call this Christmas, and it is the longest night of the year. The festivities of Yule originated back to the Norse people for whom this time of year was for feasting, merrymaking, and, depending on what was believed, sacrificing.

The Wiccans celebrate by decorating a tree, caroling, drinking, and spending time with their loved ones. According to Julius Caesar, this was the time of year where the Druids would sacrifice a white bull and collected mistletoe for the celebration.

In Wicca traditions, Yule is celebrated from back in the Celtic legend of the Holly King and the Oak King. The Oak King represents the light of the new year, and the Holly King is the symbol of darkness. The ritual is when the Oak King tries to take over the Holly King.

Imbolc/Oimelc

This holiday falls on February 2nd and is the first of the three festivals when the Earth starts to replenish the goods. Egyptians thought of this holiday as "the Feast of Nut". Nut's birthday fell on February 2nd and was seen as a mother figure to the sun God Ra according to the book of the dead. Nut took the form of a scarab beetle and, at the dawn of February 2nd, was known as Khepera. Ireland converted to Christianity, and the church allowed them to worship the goddess Brighid because the Irish found it difficult to get rid of their old gods. Brighid is viewed as the woman aspect of the "maiden/mother/crone" cycle in Wicca and Paganism.

The ritual consists of leaving a piece of their clothing outside for Brighid to bless the day before February 2nd. People put out their fire and make sure the ashes are flat and smooth. In the morning, there should be a symbol or sign that Brighid has left behind if she had passed by the campfire that was made.

If the sign is there, Wiccans would then bring their clothes back inside as they would then have protection and healing powers thanks to the blessing of Brighid.

Ostara

Depending on which day the spring equinox falls on, this day start on March 1st, 2nd, or 23rd. This day is known as the second of the three spring festivals. The word **Ostara** originated from

Eostre, who is the Germanic goddess of spring. It's the same day as the Christian Easter celebration, and also what we would call Easter, and at this time, the Jewish Passover takes place. This holiday is one of the "new" holidays for Pagans and Wiccans, because the Pagan Germans and Celts did not celebrate this holiday.

The March Hare was a symbol of fertility and growth in the medieval cultures in Europe; this is because mating season happens in March for rabbits, and they all come out in the day when they usually only come out at night.

Beltane

The third of the three spring festivals falls on May 1st, and it has been celebrated for centuries. It means that summer is right around the corner. This is when fire rituals happen, and it stems back to the Greco-Roman religions. It is fertility month, and the Celts honored this date by giving their gods gifts and peace offerings. Their cattle had to walk through the smoke of the balefires for fertility and health blessings. In Wicca, a Beltane ritual involves fertility symbols, including the Maypole dance. The pole consists of flowers and ribbons that are woven by the dancers. By the end of the dance, the ribbons are intricately woven together to form a pretty pattern. May 1st first represents the endless circle of life bringing birth, growth, death, and rebirth to life.

Litha/Midsummer (Summer Solstice)

Depending on which day the summer solstice begins, this day falls on June 21st or 22nd. Many cultures have celebrated this day as the first day of summer, and it is a celebration to balance the light and dark.

The Oak King is seen as the winter to summer solstice ruler, whereas the Holly King is seen as the summer to winter solstice ruler.

Midsummer, or Litha, is a time when Wiccans would light fires on high hilltops to honor the space between heaven and Earth. In other religions, it is a battle between light and dark. On the first day of summer, the Oak King wins the battle for power, but by the end of summer and by the beginning of the winter solstice, the Holly King takes the power back.

Lammas/Lughnasadh

This holiday falls on August 1st, and it is thought to be the celebration of an early harvest. In some religions, this day is used for worshipping Lugh, a Celtic god of craftsmanship. Lammas is the first of three harvest Sabbats and defines the time between late summer and early fall. In modern days, we do not understand the hard work and survival that our ancestors had to undergo. For us, we go to the store to buy bread, and if we run out, we just return to the store. August 1st represents life and death for our ancestors, as they had to make sure that the first grain was cut, and then the wives had to make bread from scratch. A lot of families would starve if the grain was cut too late or too early. This is a day to give thanks and recognition to our ancestors, as they are the reason we have food on our tables today.

Mabon

Mabon is what we call "thanksgiving", and it falls on September 21st or 22nd, depending on the fall equinox. It is a reminder to us that the long days and hot summer weeks are about to end, and the long winter nights are right around the corner.

This is a time when there is an equal amount of light and dark, which is why we give thanks to all that we have to our crops and harvest. We celebrate the gifts of nature and Earth, while at the same time coming to an acceptance that the soil is dying as the days get colder. In many Wiccan religions, this ritual consists of giving food and harvest to those less fortunate.

This time of year is about the celebration of the harvest and kinship, but also about the balance between light and dark, as the darkness of the moon and the light of the sun are equally balanced.

Samhain

In modern times, we call this day Halloween, and it always falls on October 31st. This holiday goes back thousands of years, and it is known as the witch's new year. Witches will contact spirits through a seance, because the veil between this world and the Otherworld is at its thinnest. The celebrations begin at dusk on the 31st, and the new year of the Celtics begins on November 1st, basically indicating that the old year has passed and a fresh new year is now beginning. This is because the harvest has been collected, the soil has died, cattle have been brought in from fields, the leaves have all fallen from the trees, and the earth is slowly dying around us.

This time of year is about saying goodbye to the old and starting to make room for what's to come. For some religions, this night is when they remember their ancestors and all that they have done, so they celebrate their memory.

The Esbats revolve around the moon's cycles, or lunar phases, and in these celebrations, modern Wiccans and Pagans celebrate the festivity with magick and by honoring their gods and goddesses. Covens usually meet once a month on a full moon to do healing magick rituals. All magick ceremonies represent when the moon is at its different stages - for example, full moon, dark moon, last quarter moon, first quarter moon, and so on. If a Wiccan was to begin a project, they would start at the sight of the new moon and continue their process as the moon goes through the stages within the month. Generally speaking, a new moon to a full moon represents the beginning of things, and a full moon to dark moon is used for the death of things, like getting rid of the negative things from your life.

New Moon Magick

This moon represents new beginnings, and so this is the phase when witches would start a project. Offerings of milk and honey or water and fertilizer for the plants is how the witches would give thanks to their gods. The goddesses associated with this moon are Diana, Astarte, Artemis, and Ana.

Crescent Moon Magick

This crescent moon faces to the west to the gates of rebirth and death. The shape of the moon means the ladle of love, manifestation, and abundance, and it is the symbol of the goddess. The crescent represents the cup of the goddess' hand, which represents the gathering of information and new ideas. The goddesses worshipped in this moon phase are Aphrodite, Themis, the Celliech, and Tiamat.

First Quarter Moon

This moon represents growth and to build upon. So, when you see this moon, it is the time to put effort into what is holding you back.

Gibbous Moon Magick

This moon is 10-14 days after the new moon and is the perfect time to make the changes you need from the previous moon phase. It's the time to either relax and take some time to think and regain energy or put forth energy into what you have been working on.

Full Moon Magick

The full moon allows you to predict the future and to protect yourself and the ones you love. Psychic powers are heightened at this time, and goddesses such as Arianrhod, Danu, Isis, Ashera, and Selene are called upon to come help you at this time. Creativity is developed, and chances of success in what you are doing is greatly increased.

Last Quarter

If you want to rid yourself of bad habits, decrease illness, and banish negativity, this moon provides you with the strength to do so. The last quarter moon represents the death of something - to banish something from your life.

Dark Moon

This phase is the most appropriate time for dealing with faultiness or anything that is against you. You should call upon the goddesses Kali, the Morrigan, the Calliech, Lilith, and/or Hecate.

Chapter 7 The Wiccan Elements

The elements involved with Wicca include air, fire, water, earth, and aether (which is defined as spirit). The elements are used for spells and are connected to every single thing that involves nature.

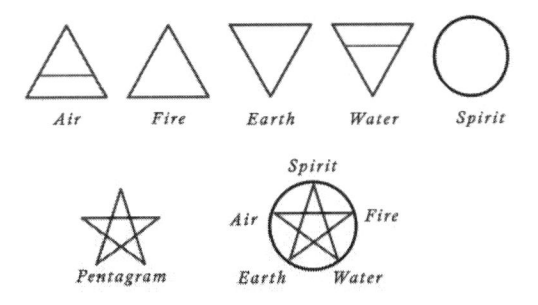

Each witch or practitioner needs to learn about and completely understand the attributes of these elements, which takes time and patience.

Air

In Wiccan magick and rituals, objects are tossed into the wind, aromatherapy is used, songs are sung, and things are hidden in really high places. The spells associated with air involve travel, instruction, freedom, and knowledge, they and can be used to increase psychic powers. Others things air represents are as follows:

The mind and intelligence

- Communication
- Telepathy
- Inspiration
- Motivation
- Imagination
- Creativity
- Dreams and passions

The symbols associated with the air element are the sky, the wind, the breeze, clouds, feathers, breath, vibrations, smoke, plants, herbs, trees, and flowers. The goddesses to call upon when doing air spells are Aradia, Arianrhod, Cardea, Nuit, and Urania; the gods are Enlil, Kheoheva, Merawrim, Shu, and Thoth.

Fire

In Wiccan rituals, witches will burn objects, use love spells, bake ingredients, and light a candle. Fire is the element of change, and it is the most physical and spiritual of the five elements. It represents the following:

- Energy
- Inspiration
- Love
- Passion
- Leadership

The symbols associated with fire are flames, lightning, heated objects such as stones, volcanoes, the sun, the stars, lava, and heat.

The goddesses to call upon are Brigit, Hestia, Pele, and Vesta; the Gods are Agni, Horus, Prometheus, and Vulcan.

Water

In Wiccan rituals, this is associated with pouring water over objects, making potions, healing spells, bathing, and tossing things into a bucket of water. Water represents the following:

- Emotions
- Absorption
- Subconsciousness
- Purification
- Eternal movement
- Wisdom
- Emotional components of love and femininity

The gods and goddesses to call upon are Aphrodite, Isis, Marianne, Dylan, Ea, Osiris, Neptune, and Poseidon.

Earth

In Wiccan rituals, it is common to bury things in the earth, create herbs, and make things out of nature, such as out of wood and stone. It represents the following:

- Strength
- Abundance

- Stability
- Prosperity
- Wealth
- Femininity

Aether (Spirit)

This element is the glue for all the other elements. It provides balance, space, and connection for the other elements. Aether is connected to our sense of spirit and well-being, and it represents joy and union. The goddess to call upon is the Lady, and the god to call upon is the Horned God."

The Wiccan Rede

The Wiccan Rede is what most Wiccans choose to live by. It is a statement that basically says harm to none, and do what you will. The word "rede" stems back to Middle English and it means advice, or counsel.

Chapter 8 Wiccan Tools Commonly Found on the Altar

Now that you have your altar set up, you're going to need some tools in order to perform the rituals. The following is a list and a description of each item you should have on your altar. Be sure to place it in the correct spot for the best effect!

Athame

Pronounced Ah-tha-may, athames are traditionally a black-handled knife; however, it doesn't have to be metal. It can be carved from wood or stone as it's not meant to cut anything in the physical plane, but only the astral plane. The athame finds its home in the East and should be placed on the east side of the altar. These knives hold the yang or God energy and are associated with the masculine. They're usually used to cut energetic ties in rituals.

Bell

Bells are akin to the voice of the Goddess and they're used to bring Her attention to you and vice versa. They're used to clear out negative energy during a ritual and to bring about healing and loving energy at the end of a ritual.

Direction Candles

Candles on an altar are meant to invoke and hold the power of each direction. Thus, you should have color coded candles on your altar. Your candles for the north should be black, green or brown. Candles for the East should be yellow or white. For the south, red or orange, and for the west they should be blue or aqua.

The center candle should either be a white and black pair or a white, silver or gold candle to represent the divine.

God and Goddess Candles

These candles can be found in the center of the altar or they can be found along the edges. You can use pillar candles, one black and one white, to represent the God and Goddess in the center. If you're performing a ritual that is more in tune with the God, you should use just one black candle. If you're performing a ritual more in tune with the Goddess, you can choose to use a white, gold or silver candle or you can use three candles – white, red and black – to represent the Maiden, Mother, and Crone.

Chalice

The chalice is one of the most important tools on the altar. It represents the Mother Goddess and is the yin on the altar. You can choose to have a very fancy chalice with jewels encrusted on it or you can use something as simple as a silver chalice. Silver is representative of the light and the Goddess, so silver is perfectly acceptable to use for your chalice. Pretty much anything that is round and curvy, even a bowl, is a good tool to use as a chalice.

Deities

It is not necessary to have a statue of any particular deity on your altar, but you may choose to have a representative of the God or Goddess you have chosen to follow or more than one. These are more than just a reminder of the deity on the altar, they are a physical vessel where you can channel the divine presence of the God or Goddess directly to your altar. Your altar will become a living temple where the Divine dwells if you choose to have a statue of a deity on it.

Libation Dish

The libation dish is a bowl or a cup in the center of your altar that will receive your offerings to the God and Goddess. You may use your chalice or a caldron for this purpose if you have limited space. When you're finished with your libation dish, you should discard the contents by burying them in the earth or allowing them to float down a river or stream. This allows them to be carried to the Divine.

Offerings

Your offerings will be placed into your libation dish. These are gifts of thanks and prayer that you may bring to your altar for the God and Goddess. Flowers are usually kept on the altar as an offering, yet anything beautiful or special to you is a good item to offer. Offerings should not be anything that could harm another thing, so flowers are usually the optimal choice. In addition, be sure it's nothing that will pollute the ground or water when you discard of them when you're finished.

Pentacle

The most commonly misunderstood symbol of the Wiccan belief system is the pentacle. It is often confused with the pentagram, an upside down, five-point star within a circle. The pentacle is an **upright** five-pointed star within a circle and is usually placed in the center of the altar. The pentacle is one of the most important altar tools as it provides protection and power by drawing the five elements together.

Salt Water

You can place this inside your chalice or your caldron at the center of the altar if you find your space is limited. Salt and water are not only used in the physical world for cleansing, but also in the energetic realm, too. Salt represents the energies of the earth and water uniting and the ocean womb that gave birth to all life on this planet. It may seem insignificant at first, but it represents so much more than just a little salt in water. It is the representation of life.

Feather

Feathers or sometimes incense are used to represent air and should be placed in the east. They are used to cleanse an area energetically and call in certain powers. Feathers and incense should be chosen according to the type of ritual being performed.

Stones and Crystals

These are commonly used to represent the earth and should be placed to the north. Each stone and crystal has its own meaning.

Wand

The wand is a masculine tool and represents yang. It should be placed in the south to represent power and will. Your wand can be made of any natural material. Wood is traditional, but it can be made of anything you'd like. Each type of wood has a different meaning, so be sure to research the type of wood you would like for your wand.

Broom

The broom is not really an altar tool, but it is used to dispense of negative energy in a sacred space. You should have them nearby your altar space and use them before and after you perform a ritual in order to cleanse the area.

Cauldron

They were traditionally cast-iron and large, but they come in all sizes now and can be as small as a ramekin. They're handy for burning your incense or herbs and is one of the reasons they're a common altar tool.

Working Knife

If you have a wooden or stone athame, you may need to keep a working knife at your altar in case you need to cut anything. Your working knife should be white handled.

Book of Shadows

Your book of shadows can be any book that has your spells and rituals written down. You're no expected to remember everything that you have learned, and a book of shadows can come in handy when you're in doubt about a ritual you're performing. At best, your book of shadows should be kept on your altar, but if you do not want to leave it there for privacy reasons, you should place it underneath the altar or in another sacred area.

Those are some of the most common items you will find on an altar, but almost every altar has an individual's unique items on it, too. Remember, this will be your most sacred place and should represent everything about you. If you find you resonate with one element over the others, you may want to have more of that item on your altar. Set it up until you are comfortable with how it looks.

Chapter 9 Consecrating Your Tools

Whether you choose to practice magick exclusively in sacred space or to incorporate your magickal practice into your everyday life, it is often necessary and appropriate to dedicate certain tools solely for ritual use. When this happens, a consecration ritual is needed to lend your items their proper intention for magickal use.

Consecrating your tools and reserving them for ritual use will keep their energies clear and focused, which lends even more power to their effectiveness in spellwork and manifestation. Furthermore, consecrating your tools deepens your religious devotion to the craft and shows the elements and gods that you are serious about your practice and are willing to show yourself and them the respect and reverence that are appropriate to a true practitioner of Wicca.

Choosing Deities for Your Ritual

Choosing deities for your consecration rituals is no small task. Some may choose to invoke the same deities that one is dedicated to for all consecration rituals. Others may choose different gods and goddesses for each tool, based on the specific use and intention behind each one. For example, Cerridwen might preside over a consecration ritual for a cauldron due to her association with cauldrons, while another goddess might be invoked for consecrating the chalice, athame, and wand.

It is important to exercise caution and respect when invoking deities for any kind of ritual. It is generally regarded as poor form to invoke deities from different pantheons within the same ritual, and it is common sense to never invoke warring deities to consecrate your ritual tools, lest your items always be at war with one another.

If gods from different pantheons are chosen for different items, it would be best to hold different consecration rituals for each tool to prevent mixing deities. If all tools are consecrated to the same deities, however, then only one ritual may be necessary—unless, of course, your guidance moves you to hold multiple rituals at different times, or if you acquire a new item after the others. Use your best judgment when choosing the deities you wish to invoke in your consecration rituals, and do plenty of research to know the best energies for each tool and the most appropriate pairings of deities in your rituals.

Invoking the Elements

Just as in any ritual, it is important to ask all the elements to be present during your consecration ritual. The elements will work with and through every tool regardless of its uses or associations, so it is crucial that they are all present at the consecration ceremony to familiarize themselves with your intended tools.

That being said, some tools will fall more completely under the domain of one element over the others depending on their uses and intentions. For example, athames and swords are associated primarily with the air element, while chalices are associated with water, censers with fire, and mortar and pestle with earth. If you choose to consecrate one item per ritual, it is appropriate to have the tool's predominant element present in a bigger way within the ritual to help channel and boost its energy into the item itself.

Casting a Circle

Casting a circle is the traditional method of setting sacred space in the Wiccan tradition. Circle casting forms the backbone of every Wiccan ritual, creating continuity and consistency throughout every spell and ritual in one's magickal practice.

Before casting a circle, it is important that one get grounded and centered to sharpen concentration and focus one's personal energy. Before working with other energies, one must first learn to control one's own energy, keeping it calm and grounded at all times during a ritual.

A good grounding and centering meditation is as follows: in either a sitting or standing position, take a few deep breaths to relax the body and clear the mind, bringing your focus to your breath itself. After a few moments of breathing in silence, bring your attention to your heart center, pressing your palms together over your chest with your elbows out. Feel the strength in your upper body as you gently press your palms together and feel the box formed by your elbows and shoulders. Next, move your attention down to your hips and legs. Feel the strength in your legs and feet, knowing that they always support you perfectly. Then, move your attention down to the ground, allowing a growing awareness of the earth beneath you. Feel how the earth always supports you, and soak in the strength and stability that this brings.

As this awareness grows, envision roots growing from the bottoms of your feet down into the earth. These roots slowly stretch down, down, down into the center of the Earth, passing underground springs and hidden stores of crystals, deep down into the Earth's magma core. As you access the molten and rocky core of the Earth, slowly begin to draw the energy up through your roots. Envision the red energy coming up from the molten lava deep within the Earth, moving up past the crystal stores and the underground streams, up into your feet, filling your body one inch at a time. Move the energy up through your legs, your hips, your torso, your shoulders, your arms, your neck, and your head. Take a few deep breaths as this energy fills you completely, then slowly return the energy back down to the earth, breathing slowly as it moves back down to your feet. Feel the solid ground beneath you. Feel the strength in your legs and feet. When you feel completely grounded and centered, open your eyes and proceed with casting the circle.

The circle can be cast using visualization, smudging, tools like wands and athames, drumming, crystals, feathers, or your hands.

The athame is the most traditional tool used for circle casting with its ability to symbolically "cut" the energy separating the mundane world from the spiritual one.

Some Wiccans begin drawing their circles in the east, in correlation with the rising sun and the springtime, while others start at the north, in correlation with the top of the compass and the north's association with the earth element, which helps to ground the energy of the circle. Choose the method that works best for you, either through consulting your specific tradition or experimenting with different methods.

Next, you'll need to draw energy down into you so that you can channel it into the casting of the circle. After you have cleared your own energy and kept it grounded and centered, raise your arms over your head. If you are using a tool, hold it in your dominant hand, which is associated with projecting energy rather than receiving it.

Draw the energy from the divine universal source down through your crown and feel it charging up towards your hands and tool. As the energy builds, slowly focus it through the tips of your fingers or your tool, slowly releasing it as you walk or turn to create your circle in a clockwise, or deosil, direction.

Chapter 10 Joining a Coven

Joining a coven is one path that a Wiccan practitioner can take. Most covens, even those that have moved away from the masonic – influenced initiation practices of Gardnerian Wiccan tradition, have some form of initiation. An initiation is, much like in most parts of the world, a secret ceremony meant to induct and admit a person into the coven. This tends to be combined ritual and screening process, as well as teaching. For most Wiccan covens, initiation tends to mean learning with the guidance of full – fledged coven members, who pass down specific traditions of the coven and teach them the "ropes", so to speak, allowing them to be able to pass muster with the rest of the coven if and when they are admitted as full members. Most Wiccan traditions also have a "lineage" or "bloodline" tradition where there are sponsors who endorse the would – be members, and these sponsors are also responsible for their guidance and teaching, becoming their mentors. The initiation process length can vary, depending on the extent of the traditions of the coven, as well as how strict they are in terms of adherence to tradition. Generally, however, initiation takes as long as it has to, until the newcomers are able to learn enough to properly participate in the communal activities and rituals, as well as fully commit themselves as becoming one with the spiritual fellowship of the rest of the coven.

Details of coven initiations are usually closely guarded secrets from coven to coven, as by its very nature it is meant to be unknown to the general public, and the details and intricacies are only known by those who undergo such processes. However, initiations for Wiccans tend to have general steps and characteristics, first being that initiation is a process, not one singular activity, as it encompasses a series of steps and activities that allows a budding Wiccan to eventually be able to learn enough to count themselves as part of the coven, and be able to keep up with the private rituals of the coven that they intend to join.

The first step tends to be meeting the coven, or at least some representatives of the coven, and being taught basic information and history of the coven, along with the traditions that the coven follows, allowing the initiate to see for themselves if the coven is indeed one that they truly wish to join. This part of the screening process may perhaps be referred to as an orientation, as this is important for both the coven members and the possible newcomer to see whether or not they are fit for each other. The coven needs to ensure that the newcomer is one that they wish to welcome into the fold, who will be capable of following their tenets and traditions, and sharing their fellowship, while the newcomer will have to understand the principles behind the coven, and understand the history, and will have to willingly choose to be part of the coven. Once this orientation is over, when both the coven and the newcomer agree that it is a good fit, the initiation process proper will begin. Usually there are assigned mentors, or perhaps the one who was initially approached or extended the invitation will begin their mentorship of the initiate. The initiate will be taught in the coven's traditions and tenets, mainly under the guidance of the mentor / s, but other coven members may participate from time to time. This initiation process can be immersive, as they need to be able to ensure that the initiate properly learns about the rituals and traditions. Depending on the type of coven, this may be academic or practical, in the sense that initiates may already be included in some activities, or in some cases, with the more magick focused covens, initiates may even already begin to participate in exploring the Craft.

Once the initiate is deemed ready to join as a full - fledged member, they are usually welcomed into the fold with a formal ceremony, where the full coven meets as a full circle in order to welcome their new member. Once fully initiated, initiates are expected to honor their commitments, show up and participate in rituals, honor the vows of secret of the coven, and be a full and active member of the support system the coven is meant to offer. Joining a coven is not a light decision, as this tends to form very strong bonds, both emotional and spiritual, among members of the group, so the one who joins needs to be sure that they are joining, as covens tend to be tight knit groups. Remember that joining a coven is not necessary to practicing Wicca, but it can be a fulfilling choice that enhances one's own practice of Wicca, but joining a coven just for the sake of having a coven may lead to regrets down the road. It is important to find the right fit for you, and in case one cannot be found, remember that there is no problem with practicing Wicca as a solitary practitioner.

Chapter 11 Becoming a Solo Practitioner of Wicca

For those who cannot find a coven that suits them, or simply wish to practice Wicca as a wholly personal journey, the choices are, by their very nature, much less clear – cut, as this becomes more personal and dependent on the person and their own preferences. Joining a coven is called initiation, but becoming a dedicated solo practitioner is referred to as self – dedication. Self – dedication rituals may resemble traditional initiation rites in some ways, due to their nature in the sense that it is about learning and self – discovery, but they tend to be much less structured, as they are fundamentally different in that one is to match the individual with the group, and the other, self – dedication, is meant for the individual to find Wicca on their own terms.

Self – dedication is a form of commitment to one's own inner self, dedicating oneself and one's practice to the divinities and deities, or to the universe as a whole, rather than a commitment to a group and a history or tradition as a coven would have it. In this case, since it is a personal journey, it takes the form of whatever makes the most sense to you, which may be very different from a coven initiation, though some parallels can still be had. For example, learning about Wicca, the traditions and the tenets is still an important step in both initiation and self – dedication, but for self – dedication, it is almost entirely driven by one's own eagerness to learn. Tradition has it that a person will spend a year and a day studying the craft before self – dedicating, but depending on the practitioner's readiness, it can be longer or shorter.

Once the practitioner is ready for self - dedication, they can begin to design their rituals in order to get in touch with their inner self and be able to attune themselves to the deities and nature, to offer themselves to the deities, in order that their understanding of Wicca and the Wiccan traditions will be deepened. Some people still prefer a more structured approach, and if needed, there are Wiccan books and even online resources that help Wiccans who intend to self – dedicate to design their own rituals to self – dedicate, or for those who are more enterprising can define or create their own rituals, perhaps starting a new ritual wholly on their own, or borrowing bits and pieces from various traditions. Once the plan has been set, the practitioner can assign themselves tasks per week or month, and set themselves goals to learn about various topics. Note, however, that self – dedication is a continuous process, where a person is constantly undergoing self – discovery and learning, so it can never really be said to end. The whole experience is designed by the practitioner, as it is meant to be undergone by the practitioner themselves. Throughout the practitioner's life, they will be the ones who have to keep choosing their path and their tasks, in order to achieve their own goals that they themselves have set. For some this is a scary prospect, but for others, this sense of freedom and challenge is invigorating. There is no right or wrong way to look at it, as this all depends on the individual and their own desires.

Dispelling common misconceptions about Wicca

Wicca in modern culture has a lot of stereotypes and mystery surrounding it. After all, it is but human nature to fear the unknown and unfamiliar, and as Wicca is a minority religion, Wiccans are prone to fall victim to misconceptions and stereotypes, perhaps even more than other religions. Wiccans can be discriminated against and looked down upon by virtue of their being different, so it is in the best interest of everyone to try and correct these misconceptions whenever possible. Here we will discuss some of the more common misconceptions, some misconceptions that lead others of more mainstream denominations and religions to discriminate or even be outright violent in some extreme cases against Wiccans.

One of the first things that needs to be gotten out of the way immediately is the fact that Wicca is not satanism. Because of the Christian obsession with witches and the strange idea that the pentagram, a prominent symbol of Wicca, is representative of the "Devil", or "Satan", many Christians, and even those of other religions such as the other people of the Book, like Muslims and Jews, have the idea that Wiccans are devil worshipers, who dedicate their lives to Satan. First of all, a Wiccan does not even believe or acknowledge the concept of the devil, much less an incarnation of one that they refer to as Satan, and Wiccans thus definitely do not sacrifice to satan or worship him. It is unfortunate that as medieval Christianity looked down upon magic and felt it was the work of the devil, and thus that misconception and prejudice has bled into modern Christianity.

Related to the previous misconception is that Wiccans use blood sacrifices, harming and torturing small animals and relishing their suffering in order to gain supernatural power. This is a great misconception, as most Wiccan rituals do not involve harming any kind of life in any way, which is in line with the Wiccan belief of respecting life and acknowledging its power and importance. There may be some fringe Wiccan traditions that make use of animal sacrifices, but this is done very rarely, and in order to harness the energy of the sacrifice, and in no instance do these Wiccans demand or enjoy any pain and suffering, and as much as possible in these cases, care is taken to minimize any suffering at all.

Wiccans are also not known to encourage orgies and sex rituals, and there may be some covens that practice some ceremonies and rituals that require one to be in the nude, to pay tribute to nature and respect our natural state, these are not commonplace, nor are they open to the public. They are private rituals and ceremonies, meant to pay tribute to nature and the natural deities, and are not some depraved ritual as popular culture enjoys making them out to be.

Similarly, while Wiccans are referred to as Witches, and the Craft as Witchcraft, Wiccans do not have a tendency towards green skin, hook noses, or massive warts. Wiccans as a general rule do not make it a habit to cackle in nasal tones while stirring cauldrons that emit a strangely large amount of steam and smoke. Wiccans are not characters out of the Wizard of Oz or fantasy tales, but for the most part, average, normal people who simply believe in and respect nature and the natural deities, and much like everyone else, simply try to better themselves and develop themselves and their potential the best they can.

Wiccan Variants

As was discussed earlier, Wicca has a few central tenets and beliefs, but there are many variants of Wicca due to its non – dogmatic nature. That being said, there are a few major variants of Wicca that a lot of people adhere to or base their own private version on. Here we will give a short discussion on a few select variants of Wicca. Note that these are not the only variants of Wicca, nor are they necessarily any more valid than other Wiccan variants, but they are here due to their historical significance or popularity.

Chapter 12 Love Spells

When thinking about witchcraft, one of the main interests for many beginners is the potential offered by love spells. The world of relationships can be tough to navigate, so the chance to give yourself a little bit of extra help when searching for a special someone is certainly appealing. For those new to Wicca, the power of the spells which you will be able to practice might not match those used by the more powerful and learned practitioners.

An enchantment for healing fractured relationships

Rather than jumping straight in with a spell to lure others into a relationship, it can be easier for beginners to focus on the bonds which you have immediately in front of you. As such, this is a great option for those who are worried about a current testy relationship or one which is going through troubled times. To complete this spell, you will require:

- Two candles (one white and one pink)
- A bowl or dish which is resistant to fire
- A fire lighting devices (matches preferable, though a lighter will work).
- Writing tools (paper, pen…)
- A length of string cut in two

The first step is to create two letters. Using your writing tools, write a pair of letters addressed to the higher powers of your choosing. This might be a god, a goddess, or another, unspecified deity. It could even be written to the universe at large. In the first of the letters, you will need to detail the factors which you regard as problematic in your relationship. Any issues or sources of disagreement are relevant, anything you might recall which causes anything other than a perfect agreement on every count. Because no one will ever read this letter other than yourself, it is important to remain as honest as possible. This may be an emotional process, but feeling sad, angry, distressed or distraught will only add to the power of the spell. At the heart of the matter is the authenticity and the honesty of the words you write.

Once these ideas have been committed to paper in the first letter, the second step is to create a letter detailing the ways in which you would like the relationship to proceed. Use your imagination to describe the ways in which arguments will be resolved and cracks can be filled in. This list can be easier to create and – while it might not seem like magic – the positive emotions which it helps to encourage can lead to a more effective casting of the spell in the long run. Once this is complete, pause briefly to reflect on what you have written and the ways in which this energy is affecting you.

Next, we will begin to actually cast the spell. Take the letter and move to the space in which you wish to work. With your letters in hand, light both of the candles. In this instance, the white candle will be used to represent the tranquility and peace in your life, while the pink candle will be used as a demonstration of the potential for love and affection. With both of these candles lit, move towards the flames. Take the first letter – with the criticisms and issues in the relationship – and place it into the fireproof container, bowl, or dish. Use your fire-lighting device to set the letter aflame and watch as the smoke begins to lift from the letter. In doing so, it will take the negative emotions with it and the smoke will begin to mix with the smoke coming from the candles. As you watch, begin to chant these words:

Sacred flames, carry these energies away,

Let my relationship begin again today.

Next, pick up the second letter. Take a second to read through the writing again and ensure that there is a firm idea in your head of exactly what you have written. This visualization process is very important to Wicca. Building up a solid image in the mind's eye is an essential part of casting a spell. Taking the two pieces of string, you will need to tie them together tightly. Ensure that the knot is as strong as possible and that you can tug at either end without the string coming undone. This knot will be used to represent the relationship as you wish it to be. Folding the second letter in half and then in half again, you will need to wrap the string around the paper.

As you fold and wrap the items, begin to chant to yourself:

God and Goddess above,

Help me reunite with my love,

Bring us loving harmony and peace,

May the strength of our bond increase.

With the burned letter in front of you and the wrapped letter in your hands, you should begin to feel the positive energy flow through your body. Holding the letter, you must now walk to a wooded area (preferably where you will be surrounded by nature) and find a tree which appeals to you. Birch or apple trees are usually the most appealing, though you will typically sense which tree is most akin to your natural style. This will feel like an urge or an instinct, drawing you to a certain tree. Once you have found it, simply dig a small hole and bury the items under the earth. As the letter decomposes and becomes one with the earth, you should begin to notice the positive emotions and energies returning to your relationship.

Increasing libido with a Wiccan spell

For those worried or thinking about their love lives, a downturn in libido can be a cause for concern at any point. As such, Wicca is one of the best solutions for restoring a bit of spice and energy to your romantic existence. Whether you are in a relationship already or are simply looking to drive your romantic energies to the maximum, turning a simple spell into a stamina-inducing, libido-increasing practice can be useful for men and women alike.

This particular spell is perfect for those who are hoping to help themselves and is intended to be used for three consecutive nights, helping the caster to make the most of their love life afterwards. Because of this, be sure that you have the materials to succeed at all times so that you will not have to start again following a forgetful night. To make the most of this spell, you will need:

- A picture of the person whose libido you wish to increase (you or a partner)
- Five candles (it is best to use four red and one white)
- A small amount of your chosen aromatic oil
- A selection of incense (choose one which appeals to the intended target)
- A small amount of fresh mint leaves
- A garnet stone (red)
- A bowl of water
- An offering bowl

To get the best results, it can help to dress yourself in the correct manner. In trying to create the right atmosphere and the right energy, dressing in red can be hugely beneficial. This could be entirely in red or simply with a hint of the color with a scarf, shirt, or even lipstick. Once you have picked your outfit, add a few drops of the oil into the bowl of water and wash your hands to ensure that they are as clean as possible before beginning.

Now, place the four red candles at each of the cardinal points (one each at north, south, east, and west) and place the white candle at the point in the center where the cross intersects. Don't light the candles yet. To the left of this white candle, light and place the incense and allow it to smolder. Take the mint leaves and the garnet stones and place them inside the offering bowl. Now that the bowl is filled, place the bowl to the right of the white candle. Finally, place the picture of your subject in the space between you and the white candle, which should be directly before you.

Next, we will create a circle of light. Beginning with the candle on the easterly point, light the flame. Moving counterclockwise, light each of the red candles in turn before finishing with the white one. After this is complete and you have created a circle of light with a central point, light the incense.

As the candles burn, you will notice that the melting wax begins to dribble down the side of the items. Lifting the white candle from the center of the circle, dribble a few of the melted drops onto the picture. Once this is done, place the white candle back in the center and lift up the offering bowl. As you look at the garnet stone and the mint leaves, picture the circle in front of you filling with a burning red light. This is the romantic color, the right shade of passion and libido, exactly what we are trying to create. Continue to hold this image in your head as the incense fills the room, and you should begin to feel the warmth of the candles filling the room and filling your body. You will need to remain focused on this energy and the feelings which it is generating in your body. As you picture this image, then you will need to utter the following incantation:

"I invoke thee, Aphrodite, goddess of love,

Awaken the fire within (name of person)

Awaken his/her desire and passion

Now and forever

For the highest good."

Repeat this message six times, all the while holding the image in your head. Once this is complete, then you need to begin the extinguishing of the candles and the closing of the circle of light. Firstly, lick your fingers and pinch out the flame on the central candle. Then, starting with western candle, move clockwise around the red candles doing the same. The incense should continue to burn as you close the circle, so take these final moments to appreciate the energy and warmth which has been created.

Remember to repeat this incantation on three consecutive nights in order to get the best results, using the same picture in every instance. Once complete, you should begin to notice an increased libido and a romantic energy in whomever is the target.

A spell to conjure romantic interest

If you are searching for romantic interest, then it might be that you are able to use Wicca to boost your chances of finding the right person. While most people would consider love spells something which is best left to fairy tales and children's stories, there is definitely something to say for those who are able to use their spiritual and occult powers to boost the romantic and positive energies which surround their love life. For beginners, the ability to cast these kinds of spells can be one of the strongest attractions to the practice of Wicca which is available. But how should you go about casting this spell?

First, it is important to note the timing of this spell. If you would like to ensure the best success for your magic, then try to cast in the first week after the full moon. Doing so will ensure that your efforts have the greatest potential to be successful. To complete the spell, you will require:

- A collection of petals, taken from a red rose
- Four candles, one red and three white
- A single glass of mint tea, brewed

Reach for the brewed tea and begin to drink it. As the tea pours down your throat, focus on the warmth and the energies which are being created within you. Finish the drink and put the cup to the side. Once you have finished the tea, begin to extinguish the white candles, starting with the one to your left, then your right, and finally the one at the tip of the triangle. Finally, put out the red candle which should still be in front of you.

Once completed, you now need to collect the energized rose petals. Pick them up from the surface and place them together in a container of some sort. This could be anything from a leather pouch to a small Tupperware container. The most important thing is to ensure that they will not spill and that you will be able to transport them. For the next week, carry these items with you wherever you go. Once the week is complete, then find a body of running water – a river or stream – and scatter the petals in the water. As you watch them wash away, you should begin to notice the positive effects which the spell will have on your love life.

Using tarot to locate a soul mate

One element of the occult which might often be overlooked is tarot. While many Wicca practitioners often forget about the ancient and magical art of using the cards to find the right answers, such an incantation can actually be a very powerful way in which to deal with the process of finding that person who might be described as a soul mate. Due to the nature of tarot, simply boosting libido or romantic energies is not entirely easy via this method, and long-term, committed solutions are actually more possible. For those who are thinking about using this method in order to find the right person, you will need a full deck of tarot cards, of which we will be predominantly using the Star, the Lovers, and the King of Cups.

The first thing which you will need to do to complete this process is to write a letter in which you will list the details of your perfect romantic partner. This can be something which you can spend a great deal of time on. The more details that are added to the letter, the more complete the description will be. Try to add in every little element of the detail to try and build up a refined idea of the significant other which you have in mind.

The things which the majority of people include are features such as eye color, height, hair color and other physical descriptions, but it is also possible to add in more abstract features such as personality traits and mannerisms, as well as skills, abilities, and hobbies. Again, the more detail which is added into the letter, the more complete the portrait of the person will be in every single way. Once you have finished the letter, fold it in two, and move on to the next step.

While it may surprise you, the next step is to enter into a state of meditation. The focusing of the mind and the energies which are present in your body will help you channel these into the placing of the tarot cards and help ensure that you can doing your utmost in order to complete the image which is constructed by the process. Relax and let your mind free itself of thoughts. Focus on your breath as it leaves your body, flowing in through the nose and out through the mouth. When suitably relaxed, move on to the next step.

Take the three tarot cards (the Star, the Lovers, and the King of Cups) and place them on the surface in front of you. Place one hand on the folded letter, and hold in your mind's eye the image of all of the characteristics that you have listed in the letter. In your relaxed state, the image should be even more complete.

As you look at each of the cards in turn, ensure that the image stays as strong as possible in your mind and that you do your utmost to focus on the idea of the potential soulmate as you see them and as you have described them in the letter. Look at the detailing on the card and try to form links between what you have described and the image which you are now considering.

As you look over the cards, use the following words, speaking them aloud:

I call upon the good spirits, I call upon karmic forces,

I call upon wide ruling powers.

Make smooth the way that my soulmate may be brought to me.

Now you must let your eyes close, leaving one hand on the folded letter. With the strong image in mind, open your eyes again. The spell is now finished. Place the letter somewhere safe and put away the cards. If the spell has been completed correctly, then you should prepare yourself to meet someone in the coming weeks. As soon as you believe you might have found that person, burn the letter using a red candle, and lay the ashes beneath a tree of your choosing.

Winning another's love with an incantation

For those times when you are have a distinct plan for your romantic involvements but need only a slight bit of encouragement, this spell can be used to further your relationship with the power of Wicca. Thanks to the magic which spells such as these possess, many people find that using witchcraft can be something which they employ for their own personal betterment. However, while these spells are not guaranteed to work, it is important to remember the power and the ability which you possess when wielding such incantations. Only use spells such as these if you are sure that you wish to deal with the consequences – they might just be more powerful than you had ever imagined. This spell works by encouraging energies within a certain person with the strength of these energies directly related to your own abilities as a magical practitioner. For the best results, try and practice this spell beneath a full moon when you know you will be in close proximity to the intended person over the coming days. To complete it, you will require:

- Three candles, two red and one white
- A small amount of olive oil
- White cloth (only a small cut is required)

First, you will need to pick up the candles and rub them up and down with the olive oil. Depending on the size of the candles which you possess, the amount of oil which you'll need will vary. Only a small amount needs to be spread, but be sure to cover as much of the surface of the candles as possible. For the best results, you should start at the base of the candle and begin to work the oil upwards, covering the wax thoroughly until you reach the wick, which must be left bare.

Once this is complete, then you will need to arrange the three candles in a line. Place the single white candle directly in front of you and arrange the two oiled red candles to either side. This should form a straight line. Once you have arranged the candles correctly, then pause for a moment and begin to lull yourself into a meditative state. Once you are suitably relaxed, you can proceed.

As you breathe in and out, begin to form a distinct picture of the person who you are thinking about in your mind. The stronger this image is, the stronger the spell will be. Feel yourself soaking and falling into the strong energies which are created by this process. With this image in your mind, keep it there and begin to light the candles. Move from left to right, lighting each one in turn (preferably with a set of matches). As you are lighting the candles, say these words softly to yourself:

Here is (person's name). This candle is him/her

This flame burns, as his/her spirit burns

If we are meant to be,

Let him/her come to me,

For the highest good,

Blessed be.

Say the words five times, considering their meaning as you do so. Now, leave the candles to burn down to their base overnight. If carrying out this spell, it is important to ensure that you are able to leave the candles in a place which will not pose a fire risk and that you will be content to leave them as they continue to burn throughout the evening and through to the morning.

After dawn, once the candles have been burned to the base, you will need to use the cloth to collect their remains. Fold the cloth closed so that the contents cannot escape and carry it outside to a wooded area. Place it at the foot of an oak tree (or a tree which is similarly long in life), and leave it in a place that will not be disturbed.

Over the coming weeks, you should begin to feel the energies as they move from the burned candles, through your mental concept of the person and into their body. During this time, you should be sure that you remain in contact with the person and that there is a suitable conduit through which the magic can flow.

Chapter 13 Wealth spells

As well as finding love, many people wish to use their newly found magical abilities to conjure up good financial results. While there are separate spells that focus on the prospect of good fortune in general, those elements of Wicca that focus on the monetary benefits that you can accrue are something of a separate category. Because of the interest and practice of such spells, we have included several here as their own category. However, far from simply being able to conjure a winning lottery ticket, these beginner spells are more likely to be able to foster a general sense of financial good fortune over the course of your life. Read on to discover how to create the best possible financial platform for your life using the magical abilities that Wicca provides.

A simple gambling spell

We will begin our examination of money spells with a look at a way in which you can improve your abilities at gambling. With a bit of added luck in this regard, you can combine a knowledge of your subject matter with the good fortune which is required to succeed in the world of betting. If you would like to improve the fortunes of the people on whom you place bets, how can you use Wicca for this end?

The purpose of this spell is to draw additional money and funds to you while you are gambling. For those who find themselves frustrated and annoyed when they attempt to gamble on sports or anything else, this spell can be a great way in which you can improve your fortunes by drawing additional positive energies towards yourself. It might be that you are playing the lottery, visiting a casino, betting on sports, or simply wagering with a friend. No matter which, the luck that this spell fosters is designed to improve your luck, rather than simply ensuring that you win outright. While you may still lose the occasional bet, you should find that you are winning and increased number of bets as time passes.

As with other spells, the best way in which to ensure results from this incantation is to use it on three consecutive nights, preferably around the time of a new moon. Because of this, be sure that you have the required items before you begin to prevent yourself from running out at any point. As a quick piece of advice, it is best to conduct this spell in the hour just before midnight and not before, as this will help with the flowing of the energies which emerge. For the best results, you will require:

- One picture of yourself (or whomever you wish to experience the good luck)
- Five candles (four yellow and one green)
- An essential oil which relates to your intended target's astrological sign
- Incense to burn (preferable frankincense or lavender)

- A selection of pineapple leaves (three are normally required, but have more)
- Three individual stones (amber)
- A selection of coins of various values
- A bowl which you can use to make offerings

To begin, you should be sure that you are doing your utmost to create the best possible atmosphere for the spell to work. To accomplish this, you can tailor your clothing to suit the spell. Green is the color traditionally associated with this kind of magic, so dressing in green can be very helpful. There is no need to dress entirely in a green outfit, but a small amount of clothing in the right color can be an excellent start. For those who do not have green available, white and black are also viable substitutes, though might not work quite as well. Once you have dressed correctly, you will need to prepare your body by washing your hands in water which contains several drops of the respective oil that you have prepared.

Take your candles and place the four yellow ones at each point of the compass. Begin at the north and arrange them clockwise on the cardinal points. Once this is done, take the green candle and place it directly in front of you. At this point, none of the candles should be lit.

Collect your pineapple leaves and the stones you have, and place them around the area that you have created between the candles. Take the coins and space them out in front of you, placing each one with care. Finally, light all of the candles beginning with the northern point, moving clockwise, and then finishing with the central green candle (just as you arranged them).

Light the incense, and allow the smoke and the smell to rise up and fill the surrounding space. As this happens, take the picture and consider it in great detail. As the energy begins to flow through you and the space, take the green candle and notice the wax which is beginning to dribble down the side. Drop several of these on the picture and return the candle back to the place where it was originally.

The next step involves you taking the offering bowl, so be sure that it is nearby when you begin. You will need to place the picture into this bowl and place the bowl down inside the circle with the leaves and the coins. Once it is in place, hold your hands before your body and say the following words:

"I invoke thee, Goddess of abundance,

Draw money and luck towards me,

May abundance flow freely in my life,

Now and forever."

As you are saying the words, you should have a very firm image of you winning your bets in the future. With a combination of the picture that you have placed wax on and the incense which is burning, the mind's eye should fall on this image of good fortune. Repeat the words three times and then lift out the picture, hold it above the green candle and allow it to catch alight. The picture will likely not burn entirely so blow on it quickly. Once it is slightly scorched and the energies have been trapped, return it to the offering bowl and place the bowl back in the area with the leaves and coins.

Now begin to extinguish the candles. With the image of winning still firmly in your mind, start with the northern candle and move clockwise around the circle, putting out the flames. Finish with the green candle in front of you. The spell is now complete, but you may keep the photograph in your home to remind yourself of the impending good luck.

Simple Wiccan Money Spell

Rather than attempting to bring good fortune through gambling, some people prefer to simply cast this spell and allow the correct energies to encourage money towards them. For the beginner, this can be one of the toughest spells to get right but also one that can manifest itself in a variety of ways. Due to the nature of the incantation, it can often be difficult to tell how the money will arrive, but faith is required in the potency of the trick to make it work. To get everything working correctly, you will require:

- One chain made from gold (could be a necklace or a bracelet)
- One gold ring
- Three candles (gold or yellow colored)

To begin, find any area of your home that is quiet and in which you will not be disturbed. For the best results, cast this spell just after a full moon. Take the three candles and arrange them in front of you in the shape of a triangle with the point being the furthest candle from you. Light the candles, beginning with the one immediately to your left and moving in a clockwise direction. Pick up your gold objects and place them in the space between the burning candles.

When your items are placed correctly, it is time to conjure a strong mental image in your head. The purpose of the golden items is to give you a solid foundation of wealth in your mind, so begin here and move onto similarly valuable objects. Do not picture why, how, or the particular details of the way in which the wealth will arrive, but simply focus on the concept of wealth itself. Keep this image in your head for five minutes, focusing and clarifying the image. As you do so, say these words ten times:

Wealth, abundance, and prosperity,

Flow into my life and set me free.

It is my will;

So mote it be.

Once you have said the words, leave the candles burning while you pick up the items from the surface in front of you. Put the ring on your finger and wear the chain. Using the same hand as the one with the ring on, lick your fingers and pinch the flame of the candles in the opposite order to the one in which they were lit. Over the coming weeks, you will need to wear these items of gold jewelry as often as possible. As you do so, you should begin to feel the energies and the sensations that are now imbued into the items. Over the course of time, you will begin to notice wealth and fortune moving towards you.

A spell for bringing success to your workplace

As well as the simple acquisition of wealth, one great way in which to improve your financial standing is to improve your professional standing. Being able to encourage success and esteem in the workplace means being able to not only earn more, but also to offer up the potential to earn even more thanks to a tremendous career. For those who want to improve their career, Wicca offers a great solution.

This spell can be used for a variety of professional purposes, whether you are searching for a job, looking to improve or increase your current salary, thinking about starting a brand new business, or just hoping to improve the fortunes for your current business. Thankfully, this spell can cover many different aspects of your career and as such, you will require:

- A picture of the person whose career you wish to improve
- Five candles (one white and four green)
- A small amount of your preferred essential oil
- Incense for burning (preferably amber)

- A small amount of bay leaves
- A pair of fluorite stones (green colored)
- A collection of coins of various value
- Your bowl for offerings

As with many spells, it can help to tailor your clothes to improve the chances of success in the magical world. For this spell, white is the best color to use, so any white clothes that you can wear will be very beneficial. Once you are ready to begin, you should go through the process of purifying yourself by washing your hands with the oil. Wash and dry your hands, and you are ready to begin.

Take the four green candles and arrange them in front of you at the cardinal points. Next take the single white candles and place it directly in front of you. You should place the incense bowl to the left of the candle where it will be easily accessible. Once it is in place, take the bay leaves, the stones, and the coins and place them into the bowl. Grab your photo and place it directly in front of the white candle.

It is now time to pause and enter a meditative state. Just as with the other spells, you should breathe deeply and focus on the spell. Now, move around the cardinal points of the candles, starting with the northern one and moving in a clockwise manner. Finally, light the white candle. Using this candle, you should light the incense.

As the white candle burns, wait for the wax to begin to melt and to dribble down the candle. Drop several of the drips of wax onto the photo using your left hand. Using your right hand, pick up the offering bowl while focusing directly on the picture. As you are focusing at the picture, recant these words:

"Success is coming soon to me,

Prosperity is flowing unto me,

So mote it be"

The next step is slightly different and will require you to sit quietly. Place everything back in the arrangement and relax, focusing directly on the money and professional success and how they might manifest in your life. Rather than simply picturing the wealth, imagine the route it will take to reach you and the process by which you will become more successful. The longer you are able to hold this image in your mind, the more powerful the spell becomes.

Once you feel you have captured the complete image of the spell working successfully, it is time to extinguish the candles. Begin with the southern green candle, work backwards in a counterclockwise motion, and finish by putting out the white candle. As you do so, allow the incense to burn slowly throughout this process.

Once this is complete, you will begin the process of improving your professional career. Due to the nature of the spell, the long lasting effects should become apparent, even if they are not immediately obvious. If, however, you do begin to doubt the process, then it can help to repeat the mantra back to yourself quietly. This will refocus and realign the energies which you encouraged.

Conclusion

The next step is to continue your work. There truly is no end to the power and experience that can be accumulated on the Wiccan path. As you continue your journey, keep this book nearby for reference and inspiration. Whether you are working with a coven or working alone, the knowledge in this book is invaluable, even to someone who is adept in the magical religion of Wicca.

Let the Wiccan Rede be your guide in life. This does not have to be just your guide in Wiccan magic but also in life. Ensure that you do no harm to others, in your words and actions. Endeavor to live in harmony with nature by ensuring that you do not tip the ecological balance. Care for the Earth and other living beings is part of living harmoniously with nature.

As it has been repeatedly mentioned in the book, a whole lot of Wiccans choose to keep their path a secret. As you must have read, there was a witch hunt in history - something that led to a lot of Wiccans shying away from sharing their knowledge and wisdom. It is therefore very understandable if you choose to practice without particularly announcing your beliefs. Today, there are a lot of negative implications that surround Wicca and the name "Witch." Since the myths and misconceptions have been debunked in this book, it would be great if you to share this book with anyone interested in understanding Wicca especially if they still have questions. As previously mentioned in the introduction part of this book, everything in this book is only an invitation that you may choose to deny or accept.

While we cannot guarantee a certain outcome, magic can increase our chances of attaining this desired goal. If you find that working alone is not yielding the desired goals, then find a coven or group to join. The quicker you find what works best for you, the quicker you will be on your way on the Wiccan path.

Wicca may have officially been invented in the early 20th century, but it has its roots in ancient magical techniques and pagan mysticism. This ancient lineage is not simply a fantasized mythological origin story, but a solid line that runs from our ancestors who practiced magical techniques to modern day magical revivals that are popping up all over the western world. These techniques are not only housed in mythology and time but also in our hearts and spirits as we navigate the modern landscape.

Printed by Amazon Italia Logistica S.r.l.
Torrazza Piemonte (TO), Italy